Tears

Become

Rain

Stories of Healing and Transformation
Inspired by THÍCH NHẤT HẠNH

EDITED BY JEANINE COGAN
AND MARY HILLEBRAND

PARALLAX PRESS

T0036718

Parallax Press
2236B Sixth Street
Berkeley, CA 94710
parallax.org

Parallax Press is the publishing division of
Plum Village Community of Engaged Buddhism, Inc.

Cover design by Katie Eberle
Text design by Maureen Forys, Happenstance Type-O-Rama

Printed in Canada by Marquis

Printed on 55# Rolland Enviro Book Natural
100 percent recycled stock

ISBN 9781952692628
Ebook ISBN 9781952692635

Library of Congress Control Number: 2023938144

1 2 3 4 5 MARQUIS 27 26 25 24 23

Contents

PART 2
Interbeing: We Are One

PART 3
Coming Home to Ourselves

PART 4
Reconciliation:
Coming Back to Each Other

PART 5
Facing Fear

PART 6
Loss and Grief

PART 7
Being Here Now:
The Wonders of the Present Moment

Introduction

SITTING IN A HOSPITAL ROOM in the summer of 2019, monitors beeping, respirator wheezing, Mary held the fragile hand of our friend Susan as she rested in a coma. It was a blow, a physical shock, to see our dear friend in that hospital room, her usually pink cheeks now pale and sunken. Her lips that had smiled so easily were now still, dry, and flat below closed eyelids that masked some of the softest, most twinkling eyes we had ever known. How could this be the same Susan that Mary had bumped into by the take-out Thai place just a few months earlier, sitting with a cup of tea in quiet amusement, fully in the present moment? That Susan, enjoying a warm spring day with nowhere else to go, was also this Susan, lying still under a thin white sheet, with a machine breathing for her.

Suddenly and literally face-to-face with impermanence, the reality that nothing and no one stays the same, tears welled up in Mary's eyes. As a few dropped to the floor, she felt herself smiling gently at her sadness and unease, the way Thích Nhất Hạnh teaches us to do, to take care of our suffering. On the way to the hospital, Mary had thought about how lucky she was to have learned this practice of smiling alongside Susan; she could now bring it to Susan's bedside, to practice together again.

One of Mary's favorite memories of Susan is of her unruffled calm during an Iraq War demonstration in 2002 in Washington, DC. As they walked together up Independence Avenue, flanked by chanting, yelling, angry protesters, Mary and Susan practiced breathing, smiling, and singing songs. They wanted to "be peace" for anyone who needed it. Singing was one of Susan's favorite ways to practice mindfulness—a soft-spoken, gentle human sitting with eyes closed, chin up, voice clear and free. So there in the hospital, Mary sang a little, and cried a little, and sang a little more, hoping Susan could hear it over the breathing machine. Mary imagined Susan, in some compartment of her brain, singing with her. "Dear friends, dear friends, let me tell you how I feel. You have given me such treasures, I love you so."

Though the singing was a breath of fresh air in that stuffy room, questions swirled through Mary's mind when she settled back into silence: Does Susan need encouragement to come back? Does she need encouragement to go? Can I be okay with not knowing? The uncertainty, the impermanence of it all, flowed back in, and when she walked out into the summer sunshine a little while later, Mary was a mess. Bicycling along Monona Bay, trying to see the path through her tears, her options at that moment were to take a break or crash.

"We have to learn the art of stopping," says Thầy, as Thích Nhất Hạnh's students call him. "Stopping our thinking, our habit energies, our forgetfulness, the strong emotions that rule us. When an emotion rushes through us like a storm, we have no peace."

So much loss, grief, fear of the unknown, and worry about not being able to do enough. Tears smeared Mary's phone as she sat down on a dock and called Jeanine. The sun sparkled on the water and ducks floated past as we shared our suffering for our lovely friend's new, unexpected state. In that beautiful, intimate moment, present together despite being 800 miles apart, those tiny drops of salt water became a soothing rain, softening the path ahead. It is a path walked by Thầy, and many teachers before him, and the Buddha himself: a path of mindfulness and compassion that allows all of us, any of us, to be peace amidst any challenge. But we must stop and look closely to see what is.

So often, we instead push away what is. We resist sitting with the present moment because what we find there is uncomfortable, perhaps filled with doubt or even intense suffering. Afraid to feel it, we may try to block it with distractions and diversions. For Mary, the cover-up is usually "What can I *do*?" In response to many such questions over the years, Susan had been exceptionally good at saying, in her marvelous, open way, eyebrows raised and eyes gleaming, "Hmm, I don't know!" Then we would set out to discover answers together.

Now, there was nothing to *do* that wasn't already being done for Susan. But there were more than enough moments to *be*. Back at the hospital, remembering how much Susan had become a part of her brought Mary tears of relief. There was nothing to do but be there, breathing together. So many times over years of friendship, Susan watered seeds of love and gratitude in Mary. These tears now did the same. Grateful for quiet time to wonder together, grateful for shared roots in Wisconsin, grateful for a loving community that practiced supporting each other by being fully present.

As Thầy teaches, clarity comes when we calm ourselves, look closely, and listen deeply. Sitting peacefully with our beautiful friend, who would have made an excellent editor for this book, Mary finally figured out what to *do*: join Jeanine on this project and, in doing so, carry Susan with us. What an opportunity to deepen our practice and create a gift that all three of us would want to give Thầy and the world: a book by regular human beings, just like us, who had been transformed by his presence and teachings.

Many of us have stories of a moment that elicited a "wow" of wonder or a sigh of relief, when we realized that we are okay—our tears have become rain. This book is a collection of such stories, with a common reason for that quiet confidence: Thích Nhất Hạnh. Some of the authors shine light on ugly truths, which readers may experience intensely. Other stories reveal humbling moments that many of us can relate to. In some stories, we can hear the authors smiling as they marvel at the uplifting impact of looking deeply at their experiences and telling their stories. Many leaned on their mindfulness practice as they dug into feelings and experiences that had wounded them deeply, even as they expressed gratitude for the opportunity to do such painful work. All stories in this collection come from authors sharing what is real and true for themselves, "like water reflecting," as Thầy says. Some authors navigated illness or other challenges while at the same time writing, revising, and answering our questions. For two authors,

Joanne Friday and Bill Woodall, their stories are among the last gifts they gave. Having died before the book made it to final publication, they remain with us in these pages.

Tears Become Rain is not full of solutions, and it does not address all of our problems. But each story illustrates a way to be okay with strong emotions, wherever and however they arise. In each story, Thầy is there, showing us that when we live completely in the present moment, we can discover the beauty of what is right in front of us and choose to water our seeds of joy.

> I hold my face in my two hands.
> No, I am not crying.
> I hold my face in my two hands
> to keep the loneliness warm—
> two hands protecting,
> two hands nourishing,
> two hands preventing
> my soul from leaving me
> in anger.
>
> —"FOR WARMTH" BY THÍCH NHẤT HẠNH

Through his teaching, his many poems and books, and Engaged Buddhism, Thích Nhất Hạnh gave his life to helping other people suffer less, even while he continued to sit with his own suffering. He learned experientially, implementing in his own life the Buddha's teachings about understanding impermanence and showing ourselves compassion. Born in Vietnam in 1926, Thầy became a novice monk at sixteen. He studied and practiced during the Japanese occupation of his country and the famine that followed. Then, while the Vietnam War raged, he combined traditional Buddhist meditation with compassionate action to care for the victims on both sides while rebuilding shattered villages. This was the birth of Engaged Buddhism.

Devastation, chaos, and death were elements of Thích Nhất Hạnh's daily life. As he described it, they were also his teachers and affected him deeply. He was determined not to hide within monastic life to avoid the violence; instead, he threw himself fully into efforts toward peace. In the midst of the Vietnam War, he lost his beloved mother and sank into a deep depression. Through daily practice, Thầy developed understanding and clarity that led him out of despair. "I realized that my mother's birth and death were concepts, not truth," he wrote in his journal several years later. "The reality of my mother was beyond birth or death." In this way, Thầy used his personal experiences to gain insight into the truth of Buddhist teachings and, in doing so, became a source of peace for himself and others.

Throughout his life, Thích Nhất Hạnh has shown us that we have the special ability—and the opportunity, if we accept it—to stop and look closely at the source of our tears. We can quietly, slowly, with our in-breath and our out-breath, peel back the figurative onion layers of our complex existence. And, just like if we were peeling a real onion, that process may bring tears; how we hold that suffering is up to us.

"The way out is in," Thầy explains. "To go back to oneself and take care of oneself, learning how to generate a feeling of joy, learning how to generate a feeling of happiness, learning how to handle a painful feeling, a painful emotion, listening to the suffering allows understanding and compassion to be born. And we suffer less."

This was the balm that would eventually soothe Jeanine's insistent restlessness, which had hummed within her for as long as she could remember. Covering it with emotional eating had produced fleeting results. Falling in love repeatedly and throwing herself into relationships had the same limited impact. Achievement worked for a day or two, but even with a doctorate in hand, her low-grade discontent remained.

Then Jeanine moved to Washington, DC and met a kindred spirit at a coffee shop on Capitol Hill. A woman with an effusive laugh and a generous smile sat at the counter talking with friends. Drawn in, Jeanine approached and said hello. Meredith, who was in love with life, offered to teach Jeanine how to meditate. Sitting with her own breath that very first time, Jeanine marveled as her lifelong uneasiness finally subsided. For that moment, and then the next, she simply followed the cadence of her breath, feeling it come in and feeling it go back out. All was still. There was a fundamental sense that she was okay as she was. The world was okay as it was. That moment was okay as it was. What a relief! What she had been seeking outside of herself was right there all along, inside.

Before she learned to meditate, Jeanine had tended to push away anything that did not appear happy. But after discovering the comfort of her own breath, which reconnected her with the joy of each moment, she began to build her strength. Like working an underutilized muscle, her breath could help her to open up and expose tender and challenging emotions she had long ago buried. Gradually allowing herself to experience her feelings, Jeanine connected with her basic humanity and learned to be present for herself both in times of suffering and in times of ease.

We know that thousands of people just like us have also been lifted up by Thầy's simple wisdom for how to live, love, and enjoy life. That is why we conceived this book: it is a gift, a labor of love to provide space for those with something personal to share. Neither of us expected what else this project became—a profound, essential practice that buoyed both of us through three years of personal and global turbulence and anchored us in gratitude during many sad and joyful moments. While we worked together and separately to guide, coax, encourage, and refine the work of nearly three dozen authors into a coherent whole, we found ourselves (by will and necessity) deepening our own mindfulness practice.

It has been an honor to be trusted by so many courageous authors. A personal story is different from fiction; it springs from our own experience, emotionally and psychically steeped in passionate purpose, and can therefore feel like a high-stakes endeavor. Our belief in the power of speaking from the heart and listening deeply bonded all of us on the path of producing this book. We are grateful for this opportunity to shine a spotlight on the art of spiritual transformation and to inspire anyone with whom it resonates.

From the start, we wanted this book to be a place for people to thoughtfully share ideas and ways to bring more peace into their own lives and into the world at a time when it seemed to be going in the other direction. Then, nine months into our first year of work, the COVID-19 pandemic turned many of us upside down. Fear, misunderstanding, and judgment swirled around the political landscapes in many countries, economies stalled, and the racial reawakening in the United States rippled into many other parts of the world. As these events stretched what we thought might be a yearlong project into two years, and then three, we saw again and again, vividly, the importance of waking up and seeing things clearly as they are. We experienced how powerfully our actions affect others. Our authors' stories reminded us of the infinite possibility of cultivating beauty, joy, and peace in all circumstances.

> If you want to cry,
> please cry.
> And know
> That I will cry with you.
> The tears you shed
> will heal us both.
> Your tears are mine.
> The earth I tread this morning
> transcends history.
> Spring and Winter are both present in the moment.
> The young leaf and the dead leaf are really one.
>
> —FROM "ONENESS" BY THÍCH NHẤT HẠNH

Thầy shared this poem, an expression of love that feels both tender and solid, as a way of holding us gently and encouraging us to be present for each other. "I will cry with you." During the course of producing this book, we received this message over and over, in heartfelt notes, short poems, and encouragement from people who believed in the project and believed in us. We are all interconnected.

As we editors adapted our pace to what our hearts and minds were able to hold at each step of this journey, we could hear Thầy's voice in the stories we were reading. These submissions were mini dharma talks, Buddhist teachings that gently guided us forward.

Several authors featured here have taken great risk, sometimes personal, sometimes professional, and because of Thích Nhất Hạnh, they trusted us. It is a testament to the power of Thầy's teaching and his many decades of community-building that these writers of different nationalities, cultural backgrounds, ages, and identities would read an invitation from two total strangers, pour their stories onto paper, and send them for our consideration. "Student of Thích Nhất Hạnh" was the only credential we needed. All of us, editors and authors, have studied and practiced in Thầy's tradition, probably even together sometimes, unwittingly attending the same public lecture or retreat but rarely meeting.

Several times, a story we were discussing turned out to be a love note to one of us editors as we cradled our own suffering. In our losses, viewed through the lenses of dear authors who had been there too, the idea of continuation was transformed from abstract to concrete. Through Jared's story, Mary started to accept her sister-in-law Carla's sudden death. While we read about how other authors faced the prospect of not surviving cancer, Jeanine held her own father and later her mother closely until they both succumbed to the disease. Through our shared practice, we found the groundedness to work with whatever life threw at us.

And ultimately, a few months before this book went to the publisher, we experienced together the passing of dear

Thầy himself. Although that event spurred us to quicken our pace to complete the project, we also had to gently release our attachment to the idea of handing a copy of the book directly to him with giant smiles and deep bows of appreciation. As our authors enthusiastically encouraged us to bring this piece of Thầy to the world, we knew these voices that echo his wise words were now more important than ever.

We can see that he is with us in their stories, and that the world needs them. All the elements of Thầy continue to exist in the way people everywhere are gently present for each other, reminding each other to breathe and go slowly. Knowing that Thầy's teachings are still present and alive in each of us, knowing that he is found in the pages of this book, we have chosen to keep these teachings in the present tense throughout this collection. As Thầy himself knew, there is, after all, "no birth, no death."

The continuation of Thầy's teachings, rooted in connection to a supportive worldwide community whom we can learn from and share with, is what we want to foster for our readers. It is why we believe this book can have immediate and lasting value, both for people who are familiar with Thầy's teachings and for those encountering him for the first time. As the stories in *Tears Become Rain* illustrate, we all have the capacity to water our seeds of joy and to tenderly hold our suffering without losing ourselves to fear, anxiety, or despair. This is fundamentally empowering and life affirming. We can make it through small irritations, such as waiting for someone who is late, and we can make it through monumental losses, such as the death of a child. As we see in each story, all the conditions for happiness are available to us in our moment-to-moment practice.

About the Editors

Jeanine Cogan, PhD, lives in the United States and has studied and practiced in the tradition of Thích Nhất Hạnh since 1996. She is a member of the Washington Mindfulness Community's Practice Council and received her dharma name, Loving Peace of the Heart, in 2009. Her name reminds her that all she needs to be at peace is connection with her own breath. Jeanine is passionate about teaching meditation to others in the community, at conferences, and in the workplace, as well as weaving it into her professional coaching with clients. A former academic, Jeanine has edited two books and written 20+ articles for professional journals. She lives with her partner, Colleen, and daughter, Nicki, in Vermont, where she enjoys taking in the green mountain views and fresh country air on daily hikes with their dog, Pickles.

Mary Hillebrand lives in the United States and has studied and practiced in the tradition of Thích Nhất Hạnh since 2001, participating in Sanghas in Washington, DC, and Madison, Wisconsin. As a high school teacher, Mary enjoys teaching mindfulness to her students and sharing her practice with other educators. In her prior career as a journalist, she has written and edited for a variety of business and financial publications. Mary's dharma name, Attentive Listening of the Heart, reminds her that, although she has often been able to impact others by using her voice, stopping to be fully present and listen can be just as powerful. Mary lives in Madison with her wife, Angie, and two amazing children, Lucy and Ben, who provide many opportunities to practice gratitude, joy, and being present together.

PART 1

The Power of Community and Belonging

My Place in the Circle

by Eliza King

"HEY, WATCH WHERE YOU'RE GOING!" the little boy in front of me snapped after I bumped him, having misjudged the distance between us. Then he squinted, staring at my face, "What's wrong with your eyes?"

The boy and I were both five years old, walking with a group of students around a yellow circle taped to the floor of our Montessori classroom in 1977.

I've heard the question, "What's wrong with your eyes?" or some variant, ever since I can remember. Born visually impaired in both eyes, I grew up legally blind. My left eye was disfigured and left completely blind after an early, unsuccessful corneal transplant. As a little kid, I had trouble maintaining a straight line when I walked and often veered into the person next to me or bumped into anyone ahead. I knocked into tables and chairs, tripped on uneven surfaces, and walked slower than the kids around me. Indoors, I kept close to a wall if I could and held onto railings as I picked my way down stairs. Outside, I usually tagged along behind everyone. That long-ago day,

I remember weaving in and out of the taped circle, unable to stay on the yellow line.

I was lucky to have parents who were determined that, as much as possible, I should participate in activities as a fully sighted child would. But even so, my limited eyesight and inability to function at the same visual standard as the kids I knew engendered low self-confidence and a sense of loneliness and isolation.

At school, I tried to be invisible, afraid to draw attention to myself by mistakenly identifying objects and people that others saw easily and recognized automatically. I did not feel I could contribute as much as other people, since I was always having to ask for help. One of my favorite classes was music, where I could use my listening skills to remember a tune and lyrics. I loved singing and enjoyed the rhythm of music. When I sang, I felt like a natural part of the world, rather than set apart and different.

As I reached adulthood, I learned to pay attention to how I felt in my body and became more secure in going at my own pace, even if that meant moving more slowly than the busy world around me. I realized that when I shared my vulnerability about my visual limitations, people were often happy for the opportunity to connect authentically and deeply.

In time, my eyesight, which I'd long regarded as a curse, metamorphosed into a gift. The way my eyes looked helped to bypass the armored facades with which most people hold the world at bay. The reactions that new acquaintances had when seeing my eyes were not always easy to be with, but they were real and authentic. I witnessed other people's gratitude and wonder for the vision they had, as well as their fear for what they might lose.

As I grew confident in listening to myself and slowing down, I also began to listen to the suffering I heard beneath my friends' and family members' surface words. I wanted badly to help them but often felt unsure how. I worried that just being with them, hearing their unspoken pain and listening to their deeply personal stories, was not enough.

One night, a friend brought me to sitting meditation at the Still Water Mindfulness Practice Center. The room had warm, orange walls the shade of a particularly vibrant sunset. A big window at the end of the space framed green leaves on trees outside. Although we were in downtown Silver Spring, Maryland, I felt we had stepped into a quiet, inviting haven.

The meditation participants sat in a circle, then afterward watched a video of Thích Nhất Hạnh explaining walking meditation. Thầy* seemed so upright, centered, and serene, even through the small screen. He had none of the overblown, charismatic showmanship I had dreaded in a famous teacher. His presence felt reassuring and full of long-lived wisdom. I was moved by Thầy's quiet but palpable joyfulness as he spoke of breathing while connecting to the earth through the soles of our feet.

I had better balance than when I was little, but I was still apprehensive about walking meditation. At first, I felt wobbly, my steps erratic, but gradually I relaxed as I felt the calm, non-judgmental energy of the group. Something

---

* "Thầy" is a term of endearment that means "teacher" in Vietnamese.

felt oddly familiar. Walking in the circle, I heard Thầy's soft, earnest voice again in my mind: "I have arrived" as I took one step forward, and then "I am home" with the next. I felt as if he was walking beside me, helping me breathe as I stepped. I enjoyed the slow rhythm of walking with a silent group. The silence helped me concentrate on my breath and feel the soles of my feet touch the smooth, cork floor.

I was delighted when I learned the song connected to the phrase:

> I have arrived.
> I am home.
> In the here and in the now
> I am solid, I am free.
> In the ultimate I dwell.

Being fully alive in the here and now with all of my fears, worries, and budding joy felt like the cutting edge of my growth. I wanted to be both solid and free, and I was intrigued at the idea that these qualities could co-exist. Learning the song anchored my longing in a beautiful, tangible energy pattern as I sang over and over to myself in the years to come, walking slowly, both alone and with others.

Upon later reflection I realized why the walking meditation felt familiar. I remembered walking on the yellow-taped circle with my small peers as a five-year-old. The difference was that now I could take my full place in the circle. I was not worried about bumping into people; I knew they would be gentle and kind, as I would be if someone bumped into me. Being welcomed into a community just the way I was filled me with peace and self-acceptance. The words "I have arrived, I am home" became true as I walked around the circle that first night with the Sangha, and they remain true today. I came full circle—arriving home in Thầy's gentle teachings, in a welcoming mindfulness community, and best of all, in myself.

Eliza King lives in the United States and practices with the Still Water Mindfulness Practice Center community in Takoma Park, Maryland. Eliza was ordained into the Order of Interbeing in 2019 and given the name True Harmony of Love, which inspires her to recognize and trust that these qualities are part of who she is. She is a life balance coach who lives with her husband and two mischievous cats. Eliza, legally blind, has learned the value of slowing down and tuning into her own voice.

Together When the Dam Breaks

by Richard Brady

WHILE ON RETREAT WITH THÍCH NHẤT HẠNH some years back, I was part of a discussion group with a woman who was having her first experience with meditation. Tears came to her eyes every time she meditated. Her life was happy, and she had no traumas in her past, so she wondered whether her situation was normal. If this was what meditation was like, she wasn't sure she wanted to continue. People responded that her experience was not so unusual. One joked gently that in Plum Village, Thích Nhất Hạnh's community of practice in France, there was a rule against crying for more than five minutes. It was fairly common, he added, to find Western visitors hidden in the bushes sobbing.

In the years since, I've often experienced intense emotions during my visits to Plum Village, occasionally accompanied by tears. Sometimes I've been alone, sometimes with others. Once, during a dharma discussion, "James" shared that ever since coming to Plum Village, he felt he'd been carrying the weight of the world on his shoulders. He could not account for this feeling. During a question and answer session the following day, James told Thầy that his brother and sister-in-law had committed suicide. When he asked for advice, Thầy responded that each of us has the seed of suicide and the seed of joy within us. Which of these seeds sprouts depends upon which is watered. Thầy went on to say that, based on what James had shared, it was clear his seed of suicide had been watered. James was at risk. He needed to carefully examine his life choices—his home, his job, his friends—and to change any elements that were not watering his seeds of joy.

That evening, our dharma discussion group met again. There were just three of us. Referencing Thầy's instructions from the day before, James shared that he had had alcohol problems earlier in his life. He felt that his sister-in-law was the only person who had supported him during this time. It was this sister-in-law who took her own life during a period of depression, leaving her husband and two small children behind. Two years later, her widower, James's brother, took his own life as well. In our dharma discussion, we listened deeply.

Following James's story, "William" told us about his brother, a doctor. Two years earlier, his brother had developed an aggressive brain tumor. William booked a flight to visit him but was then told by his brother, whose mood the tumor had darkened considerably, not to come. Ticket in hand, William decided to ignore his brother's wishes. At the end of a long flight, William was met by his grief-stricken, now-orphaned nephew. William's brother, pessimistic about the future of the world, had killed his wife and then himself.

Our dharma discussion group fell into an extended period of silence. Tears were flowing. As Thầy teaches, the roots of our ancestors' joy and suffering are within us. In our dharma group, we were experiencing that truth. Our suffering was not just personal, it came from our ancestors as well. From them we had learned to hide suffering behind stern and proper behavior, holding it at bay by living lives protected from feeling. Now this suffering burst into the open. It was inescapable. We held immense suffering, knowing it was on behalf of those who came before, on behalf of future generations, and for ourselves.

I then shared the story of my younger brother, Bob, my only sibling. As a teenager, he had a series of physical and psychological problems. Eventually Bob's condition caused him to drop out of school, and he left our home in Illinois for California, where he hoped to regain his health. Attracted to the idea of fasting to cleanse his body of toxins, Bob began a supervised water fast at a health center. After 45 days, the medical staff advised him to stop, but he did not follow their advice. He continued for fifteen more days. Two days after completing his fast, Bob went into a coma. He eventually emerged with a stiff hip and brain damage that severely impaired his short-term memory and left him subject to seizures. Since then, Bob has lived with our parents and in several communities for people with mental disabilities. He refers to his first life, his death, and his second life.

Sharing with James and William was the first time I'd told my brother's story and been able to feel my grief fully. A dam inside of me had broken open.

Through our tears, the three of us contacted a truth beyond our suffering. We had learned from Thầy to embrace and cradle it the way we would a crying infant. When suffering comes up, I feel it in my body: sometimes in my gut, sometimes my head, and often, such as this time, in my heart. As I breathe in, I speak to my pain: "Hello, my pain. I feel your presence." As I breathe out, "I am here for you."

We were in Plum Village, home to many joyful monks and nuns, Vietnamese refugees who had experienced tremendous suffering in their lives. Thầy had shown them how to water the seeds of joy as well as how to hold their suffering. In the depth of our connection with them and with each other, we found ourselves touching our own seeds of joy. Whatever liberation we achieve through our practice, we also share with the next generation. James shared the seeds of freedom and joy with his young niece and nephew, as well as with his own son; William with his son and grown nephews; I shared them with my daughter.

Twenty-seven years have passed since this experience. The process of opening to suffering has been a slow one for me. Deeply touching my own suffering or that of others has not been easy, especially not by myself. Sometimes, when I have held current emotional upheavals with awareness, doors have opened to old pain. Tension in my body has also connected me to old fears and old anger. With help, I learn to be with both old and new suffering in an accepting way—I learn to hold suffering with the help of my ancestors and descendants, for all of our benefit. It is their suffering as well as mine, a part of all of us. We can try to deny, avoid, or fix it, or we can accept it with compassion. Choosing compassion, I feel lighter and happier.

Richard Brady lives in the United States and practices with the Washington Mindfulness Community, which he co-founded in 1989, and with the Mountains and Rivers Mindfulness Community in Vermont. Richard was ordained into the Order of Interbeing in 1992 and given the name True Dharma Bridge, which reflects his lifelong efforts to bring Plum Village teachings to the educational community. Richard received the Lamp Transmission as a Dharma Teacher in the Plum Village tradition in 2001. He is the author of *Walking the Teacher's Path with Mindfulness: Stories for Reflection and Action,* and his book *Short Journey Home: Life Lessons from Thich Nhất Hạnh* will be published by Parallax Press in 2024. Richard's brother, Bob, who is a focal point in this story, passed away peacefully on November 4, 2021, after living with brain damage for fifty-three years.

Mother's Bones, Father's Heart

by Camille Goodison

IN THE SPRING OF 2014, I was at one of the lowest points of my life. I'd survived a fierce mob bullying campaign at work, but it left me sick and disabled. The unrelenting stress of a violently racist workplace manifested in a host of physical ailments. By the time I took leave from my position as an English professor that June, I had gone from being an avid runner and fitness fanatic to a woman who had difficulty walking. I knew I needed to remove myself from the toxicity surrounding me. I needed to regain my health and strength. How I would do that, I wasn't quite sure.

What I have wanted most in my career is to share my joy of learning. Entering the education profession in 2007 at one of the country's largest public universities, I approached my job with a great deal of enthusiasm and idealism, largely based on my own mostly positive college experience. Many of my students were like me: ambitious, practical children of immigrants. These were working class people who knew what it meant to struggle, just as I did. As their teacher, I wanted to give them all that I could.

I didn't want them to leave college feeling they had been short changed or had missed out on opportunities. I threw myself into my work and put in long hours, expecting little in return. I felt truly honored to be in my position, and I enjoyed my students. They possessed a sincerity and drive that I admired and found inspiring. In a few words, I loved teaching college students.

Away from the classroom, however, a different side of academia came into view. I had sensed trouble from the first day of work but didn't give it much thought. I'd entered a politicized workplace made up of faculty divided on the basis of age, gender, and race. Entrenched, systemic racism stretched back to a bigoted college president from decades earlier, and Black faculty and staff were often scapegoated for administrative failures. It never occurred to me that doing my job well and finding great joy in it would make me a target for abuse, but a campaign of racial and sexual harassment that began on my very first day only intensified over the next several years.

There were whispering campaigns to the higher-ups in the administration and among the more senior faculty that I was not the nice person everyone thought I was. Anonymous reports were slipped into my personnel file saying that I was a poor worker, unqualified, mentally ill, and needed professional help. Friends and family reported that all sorts of things were being posted about me online, words that questioned my character and my abilities as a teacher. I would get supposedly professional emails from co-workers addressed to "Bootylicious." Sexually explicit material was pinned to my office door. Anonymous mail arrived, telling me why I should quit.

After five years of this grueling mob campaign, I was so damaged that I became very ill. I felt very isolated; it was as if I had a contagious disease that no one wanted to catch. I blamed myself for getting sick, for crying every day, for struggling at work. As I write this, I am still in recovery for PTSD and a host of physical ailments brought on by stress.

I have learned that removing oneself, whether for the short-term or long, permitted or not, can be the healthiest response to a toxic situation. But in 2014, it was one of the hardest choices I could make. If I had to seek a professorship elsewhere, I wanted to do so from a strong position, not from a place of no choice and ill health. I was determined to recover first, some way, somehow. I had to.

Thích Nhất Hạnh teaches that we must sometimes go away and take care of ourselves if we are to live in community and be able to take care of both ourselves and others. I did not know about Thầy in 2014, but my Episcopalian upbringing drew me toward the idea of a retreat. Looking online, I didn't see any Episcopalian or Catholic retreats close to home, but I found something that sounded similar: the Plum Village Sangha's five-day retreat at Blue Cliff Monastery, a bit more than an hour away in upstate New York. And this retreat was specifically for people of color—a phrase I was clueless about at the time. I also knew almost nothing about Buddhism, meditation, or Thích Nhất Hạnh. I'd heard of him perhaps once or twice in passing, I think when I read books about Martin Luther King, Jr., who had nominated Thầy for the Nobel Peace Prize.

On the train up to Blue Cliff, I made a new friend who was also headed to the retreat, and for some of the same reasons. We were both professors in New York City, both from immigrant families, and both thoroughly burned out from the microaggressions many women of color face on the job. Arriving at Blue Cliff, I settled into a dorm with four women: all people of color, all from New York City—just like me. Once I realized what it meant to be at a retreat with all people of color, I felt a great relief. I felt taken care of, seen, heard, and grateful beyond measure for the attentiveness to each of our suffering and the determination to address its causes and conditions. I'd lucked into something very precious: a place where space was made for me.

My roommates had more experience with Buddhism than I did, so I followed their lead and soon learned to be still. I was an insomniac, never going to bed before early morning. In my pre-retreat life, my day never moved fast enough; I felt the need to fill each moment with activity, even if that activity was simply worrying, or eating when I wasn't hungry. But time slowed down considerably at Blue Cliff, and I had to adjust. Quiet or having nothing to do had always scared me; I felt I was falling behind or being delinquent, or lazy. But here, on retreat, doing nothing was the whole point. There was no need for guilt. All the other retreatants were doing nothing also.

After the first four mindful days, it was obvious that things would never be the same again. Away from my job and my day-to-day life, I had actually come home.

Near the time of this retreat, Thích Nhất Hạnh had had a stroke, and I realized that I would likely never meet him in person, as so many on the retreat already had. I was sad about that until I realized that the monastics taking care of me were all little Thầys, trained and taught in his way of generous peace. They met me with patience, caring, respect, and gentle humor. I was starting to feel safe.

With the aid of Thầy's teachings, the support of his disciples, and the Plum Village Sangha, I began to gain insight into the causes and conditions of my suffering. At the heart of my insight was a basic premise: everything has a cause. For me, this simple fact was a revelation: *Everything has a cause.* I didn't have to feel freakish or so alien. I had every right to be here, not just at this retreat, but in my profession and on this planet. Not knowing this—not knowing that I belonged—was the root cause of my anxiety.

My burnout had a cause, too. I had been laboring under the false notion that I wasn't enough and could never be enough. Living and practicing in community with other people of color for five days, I learned that my emotional responses to racism were normal and not indicative of anything wrong with me. As one of many people who had experienced systemic racism, I learned about the larger historical forces that contributed to my suffering. I connected with the roots of my suffering, suffering that had been inherited over generations—these roots turned out to be very deep.

I was born and raised in the Caribbean. My family moved to New York City from Jamaica, West Indies, when my sisters and I were teenagers. We made the usual sacrifices of working hard, scrimping, and saving, in hopes of getting an education and a decent shot at life. I adjusted to life in the big city as best I could. But moving to the United States, I struggled with experiences of racism. In the Caribbean, there is colorism and racism and other -isms too, but there I had the support of close, loving family and friends.

In the States, I felt I was on my own. A very sensitive child from infancy, I developed some anxiety around being a minority in a culture that didn't always seem to understand me. I learned to feel there was something wrong with me. If only I were this way and not that, if only I did this and not that, then, surely, I wouldn't be anxious. The critical self-talk was sharp and constant.

At Blue Cliff, I had both the space and the support I needed to rediscover my connection to my family and my roots. Besides holding so much suffering, the generations that came before me also created causes and conditions for me to develop a practice to help myself. The ease with which I began meditating and studying Thầy's teachings, for example, may have come from the seeds planted by my father's sixty-plus years of wholehearted meditative practice. Although my emotional struggles echoed the struggles of my mother, she nevertheless provided a powerful example of strong faith and tireless energy. Despite life's challenges, she met each day with a steadfast belief in love through activity.

Thầy teaches us to come home to our true selves. For me, this meant mindfully tending to my mother's bones and my father's heart, that is, tending to this very body that I occupy. In dharma-sharing sessions at Blue Cliff, I learned how to do this by listening to others. I enjoyed hearing what they had to say about their lives. I equally enjoyed the occasional silences, during which there was no pressure to speak. I listened, also to the silence. I sat with others' pain and with my own; this was tenderizing. The hard shell that I'd developed trying to fight off constant attacks over many years softened considerably. This process reacquainted me with the person who most felt like home: that shy, sensitive girl and young woman I had known who was kind, loved smiling, and rejoiced in the simpler things in life. It was wonderful to meet her again. I saw her in the mirror and in the open faces of all the gentle people around me.

Being deeply in touch with my true self in the present moment includes time resting, walking, talking with my niece, listening to my students, doing something, doing nothing. I no longer have to attach a material value to my every thought, word, and deed based on how much what I give can be monetized in academia or how readily these acts can be classified as a productive commodity. I know now that, with the strength and the support of my ancestors and my Sanghas, I can stay connected to my calling as an educator, even in a hostile and toxic work environment. This journey, which began in pain, has led me to a place of understanding and gratitude for what true love means—as Thầy taught, it starts with love for myself.

Camille Goodison was born and raised in Kingston, Jamaica, and now lives in Brooklyn, New York. She practices with the St. Mark's Community of Mindfulness in Manhattan, the Rock Blossom Sangha, and the Love Circle Sangha for people of color in Brooklyn. Camille says her dharma name, Deep Awareness of the Heart, given to her by the monastics at Blue Cliff Monastery, supported her budding aspirations to practice and to realize her bodhisattva vows. She teaches at the New York City College of Technology at the City University of New York and is the author of the short story collection *Chance Wanderer and Other Tales of Hunger* from Cat in the Sun Books, part of the Redux Consortium of publishers.

Wandering Along Like a Masterless Samurai

by Gary Gach

WALKING FROM THE BUS STOP to the Berkeley Community Theater in California, moving through the cool, moonlit night, I sensed who Thích Nhất Hạnh was before I laid eyes on him. I felt the open-heartedness of the throng on the street, more and more of us headed the same way. My general impression of people like me, leading a life of quiet dignity and gentle activism, felt rather nice.

At the door, the volunteers had a friendliness that easily rubbed off on me. I found a seat close to the front, grounded myself in my breath, and soon felt silent warmth spreading from the stage as brown-robed monks and nuns filed in from the wings and took their seats. Having previously lived and practiced mindfulness with others, I knew that in witnessing his community of spiritual practice, I was already glimpsing the teacher.

Thầy made his entrance stage left, unannounced. I've heard his general demeanor described as a cross between a butterfly and a water buffalo. This is true. He walked slowly, with graceful deliberation, to the dais. Along with everyone else, I rose to my feet in respect. He sat down. We all sat, together.

At first, I thought Thầy didn't seem particularly striking or special. Then I noticed that, through his calm, sure steps, he was communicating that he was completely present, from scalp to toes. Of course, a golden retriever is also completely in the now, as is a jewel thief. Thầy's particular ability to be present exuded reverence for life with deep wisdom and compassion.

What that evening has meant to me is bound up with my own story. Until then, I had wandered along like a masterless samurai. It didn't occur to me at the time, but I was possibly one of the most dangerous people in the world. I was operating on mere memories of previous teachings, without a trusty mentor in the here and now. I risked mistaking "the way" as whatever felt good—risked the danger of only fueling my foolish, self-centered ego further, driven by a wish to be free from its jealous and constricting grip.

Before this evening, I had been taking instruction wherever I found it. I had learned basic meditation from a mail-order booklet that cost me a nickel. A stranger on a bus gave me an illogical Zen riddle, called a koan, designed to crack through our ingrained, rigid sense of self, so we can see for ourselves the rich openness of life. After a talk at a small bookshop on Sunset Boulevard, Paul Reps, a spiritual teacher and artist I much admired, briefly befriended and encouraged me. In San Francisco, Katagiri Roshi trained me in formless, silent sitting in open awareness, called shikantaza. And I eagerly attended talks by Suzuki Roshi at America's first Zen monastery just outside San Francisco.

Through all of that listening, learning, and practice, however, I resisted following one guide. That, to me, would mean joining something, which went against my grain as a deliberate loner. That evening with Thầy in Berkeley, however, loosened the knot of my self-imposed isolation. The practice of mindfulness he shared would teach me how to recognize, understand, and untangle my aloneness, and it would allow me to embrace my common humanity.

I remember my quiet surprise that night. Sitting in silence all together, I felt a rare, uncanny affinity—between Thầy and his monastic community, and with those of us in the audience. I hadn't come here seeking a spiritual teacher. I was just curious. But then, curiosity has always been integral to my journey. Finding a teacher that night without seeking one was thus all the more pleasurable. Isn't life like that sometimes? Now and then, we find something we hadn't thought was missing only after we've finally given up searching for it.

It all fit. I tried doubting it, the equivalent of pinching myself to make sure I was not dreaming, but no, this was real. It was happening—and it was a great relief. I was ready, and the teacher appeared. This wasn't a mere slogan. This was it. I'd always been on the lookout for not just spiritual light but human warmth. That night, I could feel it all around me. It felt like coming home.

Another factor, similar to warmth, that I'm sensitive to is how a person speaks. The content of their speech is not the only thing that matters to me. If the speaker sits twisted, or cannot speak from below their collar bone, or doesn't pause to breathe, it's hard for my heart to hear them. Thầy is one of those rare human beings in whom body, speech, and mind are one. Right off, he woke up the room with a most memorable opening line. Looking out into the faces of 3,500 people, a gentle grin on his face, he said, "I see some of you are not smiling!"

As the evening progressed, his tone remained a consistent, enthusiastic whisper. Indeed, he was so soft-spoken that I found myself leaning in, but not just to hear. I was in awe at the care with which he formed each word; he treated words as Buddhas, attentive to the silence and space around each one. At a couple of points in the evening, some of those words crept up onto my shoulder and whispered directly into my ear, saying exactly what I needed to hear at that point in my life.

There was another teaching in how he spoke. When Thầy speaks—from the heart—his listening, to himself and to the room, encourages us to listen deeply too. "Evenly distributed listening," someone once called this phenomenon. Back then, I had been in the bad habit of finishing other people's sentences. Suddenly, here with Thầy, I was listening without letting my thoughts interrupt or interfere. I could feel myself listening both with and to my own open heart. It felt grand—and like quite a relief. That night, true communication took place.

In such communication, I touched community—a harmonious community of the selves within me and the folks all around me, people in skirts and jeans, sweaters and parkas, just like me. I felt as if I could spend the rest of my life with these people as my spiritual friends. At the talk's end, I headed out, in tandem with others. Many of us were walking back home in community—as a community— now cells of a single body, vaster than our comprehension.

Gary Gach lives in the United States and is the founder of the Zen Mindfulness Fellowship in San Francisco. He was ordained into the Order of Interbeing and given the name True Platform of Light. Gary teaches Zen at the University of San Francisco and is the author of numerous books, including *Pause, Breathe, Smile* and *The Idiot's Guide to Buddhism*.

Insight Like a Mirror

by Karla Johnston

"YOU KNOW, LALA, THIS MINDFULNESS PRACTICE really helps me slow down and remember to breathe."

I, Lala, ask my 27-year-old nephew if I may take his hand. "Sure can," Fabio answers gently. My hand slides inside his, and the other rests on top, like a sandwich. We're sitting on a garden bench just outside my mother's living room window. It's late, near midnight, hot and humid. The fireflies have long completed their brilliant display.

This bench is where I used to sit with my father, also holding his hand, many years ago. Fabio sits to my left, exactly where my father used to sit. I can feel the wooden slats beneath me bend and sag toward my nephew. My father was a big man, and the wood remembers.

I look at Fabio's hand: wide, large, and rugged. It fits his six-foot frame. His fingers are long like my own and very unlike my father's fingers, which were short and pudgy. Nonetheless, deep inside, Fabio and my pop share a similar struggle, though my nephew's situation is far more dire.

With my practice and the support of Thích Nhất Hạnh's teachings, I feel more capable, more hopeful than

I did when I went through this with my father. For this, I'm eternally grateful. I experience in that very moment on the bench with Fabio the enduring love of father, daughter, and beloved grandchild. I think of my nephew's children, all of us interconnected, and breathe in and out, recalling Thầy's wisdom. I know my family is in a moment of transformation, not just for Fabio, but for his children and for his departed grandfather.

My eyes travel up my nephew's arm, to the bruised veins. I tenderly move one hand there. I breathe, he breathes. We sit, hand in hand.

"I can't do this. I gotta get into rehab, go someplace other than Nana's." Fabio minces no words, goes straight to the heart, which is one thing I've always appreciated about our bond. He bends over, awash in shame, head hanging so low it almost touches his long legs.

"Then let's make it happen. What do we need to do?" I ask.

Fabio lifts his head and looks at me, his eye bottomless. I hold his gaze, don't look away, breathe. "Tell me what I can do for you."

"I just don't want to be alone," he says.

"You are never alone, that's impossible." I actually smile through the heartbreak. Fabio's not in the mood for existential Ultimate Dimension talk. I try again, "Let's make sure that doesn't happen then."

The next two weeks present the practice opportunities of my lifetime: Fabio's relapse and homelessness, my own all-nighters, and days spent literally by my nephew's side until he finally settles into a rehabilitation center that's a good fit. Moment by moment, we actively practice being present with his addiction. I cannot tell you how many times I think, what would Thích Nhất Hạnh do? What would he say? How many times I remember and draw from the energy of Sangha, my treasure trove of wisdom and insight. As I sit in the emergency room with my nephew days after an attempted overdose, again holding his hand, encouraging him to breathe, to be still, and to not rip off his hospital bracelet and run, I never doubt that Thầy would approve.

Bodhisattvas near and far join us in care: a nurse who unlocks the hospital cafeteria, only open to staff, at 1 a.m. so we can eat after being told, "we have no mental health bed available." The inner-city McDonald's workers who bring Fabio and me drinks as we sit together on the curb in the hot sunshine when he refuses to go inside. The young man who comes up to Fabio, shakes his hand and says, "I believe you struggle with the same thing my brother struggled with. You've got to be strong, every day. You can do it, man!"

Mysteriously, I was invited to bring the practice of mindfulness to a local treatment center, Elevate Addiction Services, months before Fabio's struggle with opioid addiction began. I was initially hesitant, as I did not have a personal experience of addiction and was very uninformed. However, I accepted the invitation and started this work, and what I learned was astounding: opioid addiction in the United States had reached epidemic proportions, with a public emergency declared in 2017. At that time, one in three people knew someone addicted to opioids. During the COVID-19 pandemic those numbers skyrocketed, and overdoses increased by at least 50 percent.

Little did I know that I was also preparing to support my own family in this struggle. In my work, I heard recovering addicts seeking to answer heroic questions: What do we do when the present moment is too painful to bear? Can we learn to put down a harmful substance and instead practice a compassionate response? What are our blessings, alive in the midst of our suffering?

The addiction treatment center became for me another Sangha, a community of practice that was literally preparing me for the journey to come. This recovery Sangha was a boat for my family and me to step into six months later, when we discovered Fabio's heroin use and began riding the storms of addiction and recovery ourselves.

Over the course of two years, Fabio's life unraveled. He spent more than two months in prison, lost custody of his children, and, most tragically, experienced the death of his girlfriend from an overdose. Yet through all of this, my nephew remained resilient and determined to move forward. Eventually, he gave back to the recovery community through a newfound livelihood of renovating and beautifying recovery homes.

My nephew's experience has informed in every way my capacity to be present for those I meet at the addiction treatment center, where I still share the practice of mindfulness. The reason I practice has changed: I have a very real, life-or-death aspiration to cultivate the capacity to listen wholeheartedly, no matter how ugly the words and sounds, and to offer what's needed most at pivotal moments.

A few days ago, after a Sangha meeting at the treatment center, a young man approached me and said, "I want to ask a question I've not asked before, but I think you'll be honest. What do you see in me?"

I held this young man's gaze and breathed with the heartache his question stirred. He stayed with the pause, even lifted his head and stood taller. As we practiced together, he did not look away. I took a breath and spoke of worth, vision for a better life, strength, and resilience. I posed a question to him, "What do you see in yourself?"

His response was telling, "It's like I'm looking in a mirror and I think, 'You forget about this guy, all the time.'" We spoke of gentleness, of insight like a mirror, and of the practice of embodying ourselves by experiencing the breath, returning to what is present with compassion. We connected deeply. We touched the preciousness of life.

Karla Johnston lives in the United States and is the founder of the Lake Tahoe Mindfulness Community and the Lotuses in the Mud Recovery Family in California. Karla was ordained into the Order of Interbeing in 2017; she received the dharma name True Compassionate Dwelling. To her, compassion is the number one condition for love and understanding. One of Karla's greatest joys is bringing the practice into rock-bottom situations and seeing relief and hope grow. She shares this joy in her TEDx talk, "Can Mindfulness Help Solve the Opioid Epidemic?" Karla has contributed articles to the *Mindfulness Bell* and authored *Child of God: The Humble Beginnings of Joan of Arc*.

Confusion Disappears
with Each Step

by Hans d'Achard van Enschut

I WAS A SINGLE PARENT in Eindhoven, the Netherlands, for almost ten years, with one daughter in university and another in high school. We had a good time and could deal with the normal struggles, but one day, my challenging and stressful job in high-tech research and development was terminated. As a result, I was dragged into a legal struggle with my employer. Being without a job turned my world upside down. My hopes, dreams, and view of the future were shattered. Suddenly the things I took for granted disappeared: my income, my confidence, and my health. I was emotionally and physically drained.

So when someone suggested I'd better take a break, I thought, *If I go sit on the beach for a week, I may be rested afterwards but nothing will have changed in me, or in my life. If I don't change, I'll run into troubles again.* I realized I had to learn something new, but where to go? I recalled a late-night campfire conversation that I'd had about eight years before, when a man had told me that there was a place in France led by a Vietnamese monk. He said the monk had changed his life. I did not know the name or address, but I found it on the internet in ten minutes. The place was Plum Village, and the monk was Thích Nhất Hạnh.

I still do not know why I made the split-second decision, but I called the number on the website without hesitation. It felt like a last resort. The friendly person on the phone listened to my story, and then I asked him if I could come for two weeks in April. He said, "Dear brother, you are most welcome. However, please note that we do not have any medical facilities or skills."

So I packed my bags, my twelve bottles of vitamins and minerals, and hoped for the best. I was so low in energy and concentration that it took me three days to drive from Eindhoven to Plum Village, a distance of one thousand kilometers that would typically take one day. During those three days on the road, I felt anxious and uncertain, but I saw no alternative; it was a leap of faith.

When I arrived, I was exhausted, both by my trip and my burnout. I had been in the habit of sleeping a minimum of twelve hours a day, after which my energy level was still low. I asked the monks if I could skip part of the daily routine, which involved rising early. The answer came as a relief, "No problem, feel at home and join when you can." I had been pushing myself to keep going, to adjust to others. Here this was turned around; I was welcome for who I was.

Plum Village, a collection of former farm houses within walking distance of each other, was a complete surprise to me. The brothers arranged for me to stay in a group of buildings called Upper Hamlet, up on a hill overlooking the grapevines in the French countryside. The atmosphere was very peaceful and friendly. Besides the sixty monks, there were not many guests at Upper Hamlet, maybe five or six and about fifteen long-term residents. Our connection was instant. From the first day, they took me in as if I were a long-lost friend. Their friendliness and warm, full attention were an extreme contrast to the impersonal climate I had left three days before. In comparison to Plum Village, my former job environment seemed downright hostile.

Miraculously, after a day or two, my energy began to come back, and after five days, I was fit enough to follow the full daily program together with the monks. Our day typically started with morning meditation in the big hall at sunrise, followed by breakfast, a Dharma talk about mindfulness, walking meditation, and lunch. Afterward, we did light meditative work in the kitchen or garden, attended a group sharing, ate dinner, and then sat for an evening meditation. What I experienced was beyond words: I felt safe, made deep connections, and felt fresh again.

The dharma talks were opening a new world for me. A monk named Cuong Lu was teaching Buddhist psychology for the full duration of my stay. I had been completely ignorant of Buddhist practice. Up until then, I had not met Thầy nor heard any of his talks, but I felt through and through that this community was inspired and nourished by him.

After several days, Thầy gave a talk about the translation of one line in a sutra, an account of a talk by the Buddha. This line was maybe six or eight Chinese characters, yet he talked about it for almost two hours. I did not understand a word of it, not even the topic of the sutra. I was stunned. I could not imagine that this was the same monk who was praised for his wisdom, compassion, and clarity.

After the talk, we gathered silently for walking meditation with the whole friendly and kind community of monks, nuns, and lay people. Wherever I looked, I saw peace and kindness. I was bathing in a sea of brotherhood and sisterhood. Thầy's talk disappeared from my mind, my confusion disappeared from my mind, and I concluded that if the energy and warmth of Thầy could build this community, this is what I wanted to learn and be part of.

My body was healing, my mind was healing, my trust in people was healing, and my spiritual connection was healing. New friendships were growing at lightspeed. I could feel myself lean back, and with the slow life and calm pace, I started to notice that spring was here: a huge variety of flowers were blooming.

At the end of the two weeks, I did not want to go home. I wanted to stay. With a friendly smile, one of the brothers advised me to look deeply into my desire to stay and my hesitation to go back. That night, I sat alone, meditating in one of the smaller and older meditation halls called the Transformation Hall until after midnight. Looking at my feelings, I saw fear of the outside world, fear of the hostile, impersonal place I had fled two weeks before. When I looked deeper, I realized I missed my daughters.

Before I went to sleep, I made my decision; I looked in the mirror in the washroom and said to myself, "Go home and come back in six months. See if this new experience is real or an illusion."

At breakfast, the brothers sang for me one of the beautiful Plum Village songs called "No coming, no going," which expresses that we share this life and are part of each other's lives. I was so moved by the friendship that I cried out of love and joy.

When I got home, I could not stop talking. My eldest daughter asked jokingly if she could help shave my head, like a monk's. After a month or two, I looked in the mirror again—looked at all the conversations I had had with friends and family since my return, looked at all the things I had read. All my feelings pointed to one thing: go back, and see if it was a dream.

I returned for my second retreat. This time, I attended the Neuroscience Retreat, an organized event with about four hundred visitors of twenty-five nationalities. Plum Village had invited all these people to share experiences and learn from each other. The brotherhood and sisterhood were there, the flowers were there, Cuong Lu was there, my new friend Gary from Canada was there. This time, Thầy gave all the dharma talks, and I immediately understood the amazing impact of his kindness and love. He spoke with patience and compassion. He shared deep insights in a clear and effective way, adjusting to our pace.

Humbly, I received The Five Mindfulness Trainings, which are a personal aspiration for life ethics, and Cuong Lu gave me the dharma name Sacred Breath of the Source, which I cherish. A dharma name is a name given to mark a new start. It reflects your aspiration and an aspect that the teacher recognizes in you.

This time, I was filled with gratitude when I returned to Eindhoven. I had the urge to share and to pass on what

I had received. I shared my experiences with my friend Elisabeth, who was the student chaplain at the local university. She was immediately curious and enthusiastic. She arranged for me to use one of the university's rooms to show students videos of Thầy's dharma talks, first monthly, but later every week. To practice and share with young people who were finding their way in life was a very rewarding experience.

Passing along the help I had received in Plum Village reminded me of my own student years and of how I had struggled to find my way. This new group that gathered around Thầy's dharma talks formed the basis of my home Sangha, a nourishing, caring, vibrant community of people now practicing meditation and sharing experiences for more than fifteen years.

Hans d'Achard van Enschut lives in the Netherlands and practices with several Sanghas, including the Mind Only Sangha. His dharma name, Sacred Breath of the Source, which he received in 2006, has been both a koan and a comfort to him. Hans is the father of two daughters, and he is a grandfather. He teaches physics to promote understanding of the physical world and the application of this understanding to improving life. Viewing collaboration as imperative in his work, understanding people and bringing them together has always been at the core of Hans's contributions. It is the reason he teaches and mentors young people.

A Handful of Salt

by Natascha Bruckner

GROWING UP, I LEARNED TO be a staunch individual-
ist and took pride in being self-sufficient. I was so caught
up in "doing it myself," so convinced independence was
strength, that I was blind to the direction I was heading in:
a narrow, rigid life of being attached to my way of doing
things, an isolated life closed off from true connection.

Thích Nhất Hạnh helped me to make a course correc-
tion with his teachings about Sangha—a Sanskrit word
that means group, congregation, or community. Thầy
taught me that we're all stronger when we join our energies
and don't have to carry things on our own.

But I didn't grasp that right away. My first taste of
Sangha was in 2001, at a retreat in San Diego. I say "taste"
because during those five days, I barely opened myself
up to the other people who had gathered there. I moved
around the retreat like a solitary satellite, staying mostly
silent and not engaging with others. Though people were
all around me, I was quite alone there.

Listening to Thầy's talks was deeply moving, and I
cried with the painful recognition that my lifestyle—the

constant busyness, the stress of trying to reach an unreach-able standard of perfection, the lack of inner peace—was causing me a lot of unhappiness. I kept my feelings to myself, which was typical for me at that time. However, in an LGBTQ dharma discussion group, I had an intro-duction to the gift of Sangha. A dharma discussion group is a small group of people who meet each day to share thoughts and feelings about our practice. I felt the warm welcome and kinship of the group, even as I remained shy and guarded. I didn't speak much, except for my nervous presentation of a poem on the last day.

Still, as others shared openly, their insights helped me understand and deepen my own spiritual journey. I dis-covered what a rare, valuable gift it was to speak honestly and to connect vulnerably with people in a circle of trust held by wise and kind-hearted facilitators. This was the beginning of my trying to heal the relative isolation that had been my normal. In this isolation, I had denied myself the warmth and messiness and joy and learning that comes from raw, real human connection.

Thầy likens Sangha to a river. Each person is a drop in the current. Alone, we don't get very far, but combined, we're able to reach the ocean. After that retreat, I worked at integrating Thầy's teachings into my life to shift my energy beyond my own little dramas to a bigger cause; the Sangha is a larger organism of which I have, since my first retreat, become a humble but necessary part.

A group called the Heart Sangha, which meets regularly near my home, provides powerful medicine that brings me peace. It is one of hundreds of such groups meditating in Thầy's tradition all over the world. We meet once a week in the beautiful Santa Cruz Zen Center. Usually there are fifteen or twenty of us.

I love this Monday night practice, which starts with a large bell sounding three times to invite us into silent meditation while we sit in a circle, facing the center. It's a chance for each of us to meditate within the profoundly concentrated energy of collective focus, which is an energy much more potent than when I meditate alone. Solo practice can be wonderful, but sometimes I am easily distracted by what's happening in my environment or preoccupied with the noise of my thoughts. When I meditate with a group, the silent stillness resounds, the peaceful energy is magnified, and I find it easier to focus and rest deeply in meditation.

For me, the sharing and connecting with others in our Sangha gatherings is a continuation of the wonderful freedom I found on retreat. Here, I share my suffering and hold that of others. We talk about the teachings, our own struggles and joys, and about whatever comes up for us as we try to practice mindfulness in our daily lives. These discussions give me a chance to speak from the heart and to practice the art of deep listening—listening without judging or interrupting, trying not to allow my own thoughts to take my attention away from the speaker. It's a time to connect with other human beings, a time to know we are not alone. And because we are there to actively study and practice compassion and kindness, our gatherings tend to bring out the best in us: they are shaped by gentleness and respect for each other.

Those Monday Sangha evenings are the grounding point, but I know now that Sangha is much more than just a bunch of like-minded meditators gathering each week. Sangha is an extended body, an ecosystem of interconnected beings, a "loving and supportive community of practice," as Thầy says. Like the cells of a human body, we are all separate individuals that contribute to the functioning of the whole. We're unique, with our own stories and opinions, but we practice mindfulness as one body. The presence of our "one body" can be felt when we sit together in meditation and a clear, deep stillness fills the hall. Our diversity makes us strong and resilient as we weave different perspectives together.

When my aunt Helen, one of my mother's triplet sisters, died suddenly of a heart attack, I brought my suffering to the Sangha. I was heartbroken. She was like another mom to me, and I loved her deeply. Since Helen lived in another state, I was not able to see her; the day I heard the terrible news, I told the story through tears and asked the community to sing "You Are My Sunshine." This was a song my grandmother sang to show how dearly she loved her children and grandchildren. My Sangha friends did not know my aunt, but they loved her because I did. As we sang together, I felt my love magnified and strengthened by their love. Though we sang to my aunt, I felt the group was also singing to console me.

In his book *The Heart of the Buddha's Teaching*, Thầy says, "If you take a handful of salt and pour it into a small bowl of water, the water in the bowl will be too salty to drink. But if you pour the same amount of salt into a large river, people will still be able to drink the river's water." The salt is like the suffering in each of our individual lives. Hearing the singing voices of our one Sangha body, I felt held, comforted, relieved. The embrace of a loving community is a balm that has healed my tendency to struggle with difficult emotions alone.

Natascha Bruckner lives near the Pacific Ocean in the United States with her partner, Zachiah Murray, and their four cats. She is a member of the Heart Sangha in Santa Cruz, California. In 2011, Natascha was ordained into the Order of Interbeing and received the name True Ocean of Jewels. She completed a chaplaincy training program with Roshi Joan Halifax at Upaya Zen Center in 2020 and a year later received the Lamp Transmission to become a dharma teacher in the lineage of Thích Nhất Hạnh. She works as an editor and finds joy in caring for aging loved ones, volunteering with hospice patients, supporting Buddhist and restorative justice programs in prisons, and crocheting.

PART 2

Interbeing:
We Are One

Holding Your Hand in Mine

by Annette Saager

I WAS A SINGLE MOTHER and had never left my daughter, Anne, for this long before. It was 2005, and I was planning to travel to Vietnam for four weeks with Thích Nhất Hạnh and the Sangha. While preparing for this trip, I was pre-occupied with how to reduce my fear, even though Anne assured me that it was okay for her, at eighteen years old, to stay alone for this period.

From my work with people who have lost dear relatives, I knew that the grief of those who did not get the chance to say goodbye to their beloved ones contained particularly potent suffering. Because of their experience and my own anxiety, I was looking for a ritual—a way I could celebrate the moment of parting with my daughter that would allow me to be more at ease.

In our Plum Village tradition, we practice hugging meditation when we say "hello" or "goodbye" to each other. In Thầy's version of hugging, we take three mind-ful breaths in and out while remaining fully present with our companion. We do not talk or focus on what might be coming up next. I have appreciated this practice very much, but I could not share it with many people in my daily life. Often, people who do not practice in this tradition do not like such close physical contact.

I try to be conscious of when hugging meditation fits the moment and when it might not. When my mother was dying, she was in a silent state, very busy with her effort to breathe. I did not dare to take her in my arms; she seemed so fragile. Sitting beside her, I instead held her hand between my two hands and breathed with her. This gave me comfort and a deep feeling of being with her. With each breath she took, I silently talked to her: "Let go." In doing so, I realized that, as her daughter, I was letting my mother go. I was saying goodbye to her.

After her death, I was sad, of course, but I felt I carried her inside of me; the deep sharing we had experienced with each other before she died helped me to feel connected to her.

Getting ready to leave my daughter for my trip to Vietnam, I remembered this practice I had relied on with my mother. In the weeks leading up to my trip I practiced this ritual with Anne each time we parted. I took her hand between my two hands, practiced being totally aware of her, and let go. This helped me to be more present with her, and she became more present with me too. When it was time for me to say goodbye, this exercise turned out to be a big help—I knew I was ready to go.

This little ritual, though, had not originated with me. Thầy had first helped me to understand the power of hugging meditation and mindfulness in 1994. As a fruit of his teaching, in 2011 I offered to him this gatha, a small poem to help with a particular part of mindfulness practice.

I shared it during our Lamp Transmission Ceremony, when I became a teacher in Thầy's tradition:

> Your hand in my two hands
> I close my eyes
> Breathing in, I am totally aware
> Breathing out, I let go
> I rest in peace.

After I recited this gatha to Thầy, he asked me if I would like to take his hand. He offered me his right hand, and I embraced his hand with my two hands as I silently repeated my gatha in a new version of this little ceremony that I had practiced so often before. Then Thầy spoke the following words: "This is a pure, true, and sincere practice. Thầy's hand is in your hand, your hand is now in Thầy's hand, both hands have met each other. Thầy carries you in his hand wherever he goes."

These words and my memory of the feeling of his hand in my hands offer me peace, wherever Thầy may be. We met each other; I am in him, and he is in me. That is inter-being, and I no longer need to fear moments of saying goodbye, to him or to people who are dear to me. We are always connected, and we cannot miss each other.

Annette Saager lives in Germany, where she is active in the Practicing Mindfulness in Marktgräflerland Sangha in Müllheim as well as several Sanghas dedicated to palliative care and the grieving process. Born in East Berlin, Annette escaped to West Berlin in 1957. She eventually settled near the Black Forest, in southern Germany, where she works in dentistry and palliative care. She received the Lamp Transmission to become a dharma teacher in 2011. Her dharma name, True Source of Virtue, reminds Annette of her opportunity to offer the practice in areas of deep suffering: hospitals, hospice groups, and grief groups. When not doing that, Annette enjoys playing her ukulele and working in her garden.

Gently Blowing Out the Fires

by Chaya Ocampo Go

IN THE ORIGIN STORY OF the Chinese zodiac, it is told that once upon a time an emperor invited all the animals in the kingdom to a race. The first twelve animals to reach the finish line would each be assigned a year in the calendar. The majestic dragon was the only mythical creature among the rest, yet she was outrun by the rat, ox, tiger and rabbit. "What took you so long?" asked the emperor when the dragon came flying in from the clouds, arriving in fifth place. The dragon said that on her way over, she flew by a poor village suffering from a drought, their crops burning in a fire. She had stopped to gather rain clouds for them and gently blew off the flames with her breath. The emperor smiled at the dragon's noble heart, feeling the same awe I did as a little girl when I first heard this story.

I was born in Manila, Philippines, soon after the People Power Revolution of 1986 toppled the dictatorship of Ferdinand Marcos and restored democracy in the country. I was raised in a Chinese-Filipino family, and my parents were the first to open my young eyes to the realities of social suffering in the country. They were active in a

Catholic ministry and brought us children along to political demonstrations. My mother worked in various civil society organizations training daycare workers in marginalized communities.

After studying anthropology at the university, I committed myself to a life of humility in service to others as a social worker at the Assisi Development Foundation, a non-profit organization inspired by St. Francis of Assisi. In a country governed by a weak state that has long relied on social workers, volunteers, and charities to provide basic social services for its people, mine was a well-trodden path. During these years as a social worker, I learned with my colleagues how to conduct and sustain grassroots projects in support of water and food security, health, education, and livelihoods. In a country of more than seven thousand islands, we traveled extensively to reach far-flung rural communities and island towns where life is a daily struggle.

In 2013, super typhoon Haiyan, the strongest storm in recorded history, killed over ten thousand people in the Philippines. In the aftermath, I worked in emergency relief amidst ravaged villages and mass graves for many long months until my heart, spirit, and body were broken. When I was offered a scholarship to pursue graduate studies in Canada, I had to accept. Leaving was my first chance to catch my breath, rest, and touch my own grief deeply. With time and distance away from ground zero of the climate crisis, I experienced the exhaustion in my body. I took time to mourn all we had loved and lost, and to accept that there is no "post-disaster" phase in which to recharge; intensifying storms continue to come, one after the other. Clearly, I needed a path of practice that would sustain this lifelong work.

I had learned about Thích Nhất Hạnh in high school and now felt drawn to his books for wisdom. It was during my graduate studies that I discovered Sister Chan Khong's autobiography, *Learning True Love.* She was one of the key student leaders of the School of Youth for Social Service, which she and Thầy founded in Vietnam during the Vietnam War. Her firsthand stories of working to rebuild bombed villages, aiding the sick and hungry, navigating political repression, and trying to end the war resonated deeply. Their experiences were similar to mine: we, too, worked on the front lines of disasters and climate change, struggling to provide swift relief while our own lives were also threatened. Later, I would find further poignant accounts in Thầy's journals, *Fragrant Palm Leaves.* Reading these books, I wept. Thầy exemplified the work of the *bodhisattva*, someone on the path of enlightenment, in the way he strove again and again to rebuild villages in Vietnam, even after they had been repeatedly bombed. In the same way, we continue to rebuild huts and lives again and again in the Philippines, even when poverty and displacement creep ceaselessly back into the lives of the people there. Thầy and Sister Chan Khong's stories were also our stories! Their path was my path.

I decided to ground myself in Thích Nhất Hạnh's community. While hearts of great compassion live in those engaged on the frontlines of social action, strong habit energies of panic, anger, sorrow, and confusion also often propel our actions. As I began to cultivate a regular mindfulness practice with the support of Sangha and mentors, I learned the vital importance of pa-hinga, the Filipino word that means both "rest" and "to breathe." Resting in the breath started to grow in me as a daily way of life. In turn, this nurtured my scholarship as well as my social-climate justice activism.

From Thầy I learned that wisdom and action must go hand in hand. This is expressed most clearly in The Fourteen Mindfulness Trainings, a set of precepts practiced by members of the Order of Interbeing. Thầy founded the Order to create a structure to support people working to relieve the suffering of others. During the Vietnam War, the Order practiced a shared Day of Mindfulness each week to rest and restore themselves so they could continue to serve in times of great destruction.

Through Thầy's teachings, the Sangha, and our daily practices, I can now touch a quiet, gentle, unshakable power when my breath, body, heart, and mind unite as one. In one of his beautiful calligraphies, Thầy wrote, "The tears I shed yesterday have become rain." Grief, sorrow, and despair can be transformed as a gentle rain of deep peace and joy for service.

In August 2019, I stepped forward with Sangha friends to take part in an ordination ceremony to join the Order of Interbeing. A heart that cares deeply for others is not mine alone, but a gift transmitted by my ancestors, parents, teachers, and friends. Seated in the monastery, I held my grandfather's prayer beads in one hand and, in the other, a memory of my second grandfather leading an earthquake victims rescue. I invited my mother's and father's two great hearts to beat with mine. My husband and mentors sat close by, surrounded by the monastic Sangha, an embodiment of Thầy and Sister Chan Khong. I wept tears of tremendous gratitude.

That ceremony was a beautiful celebration of the best our human hearts can vow to cultivate and offer in these turbulent times. The bodhisattva vows to serve all beings in a world on fire and to hold wisdom and action hand in hand. Like the dragon's noble heart in the ancient Chinese myth, we are all of the nature to live with boundless compassion, to blow out fires with our own gentle breaths, and to shower our tears like rain where the land is parched.

Chaya Ocampo Go lives in the Philippines and serves as the co-chair and a Care Taking Council member in the Earth Holder Community, a Plum Village Sangha for earth justice. She was ordained in the Order of Interbeing in 2019 and given the name True Radiant Cloud. She views this name as an invitation to live with beauty and freedom, to see her continuation in many forms, and to not be caught in the need to control the outcomes of any action. As a cloud becomes rain and flows into rivers, to trees, gardens, and the earth, so does she. Chaya completed a doctorate in critical disaster studies at York University and is exploring ways to contribute to social-climate justice work in the Asia-Pacific region. A mother of two little ones, she is of Filipina-Chinese heritage.

Thầy in Disguise

by Vickie MacArthur

MY HEART FELT TENDER AND RAW. I had spent the past three months sitting by my mother's bedside in palliative care, watching as the tumor that began in her right ovary slowly but relentlessly extinguished the spark of life in her clear blue eyes. My life had been a blur of both busyness and being: packing away a lifetime of memories in my mom's home as we moved her into palliative care; endless doctors' appointments and tests; quiet moments of holding her hand and watching her breathe; and, finally, planning her funeral and attending to the myriad details that accompany the grief of losing a loved one. My heart felt as fragile as my mother's fine crystal, which I had hurriedly boxed away in my garage.

So when I attended my first retreat with Thích Nhất Hạnh in Vancouver, Canada, shortly thereafter, I simply wanted a refuge, some quiet time to sit and unpack my feelings of sadness and grief. Towards the end of the retreat, I had the opportunity to sit quite close to the beloved Buddhist master. I looked up, and it felt like his eyes were drawing me in; his all-encompassing gaze seemed to hold the depths of my soul. Time seemed to stop. Everyone and everything else in the room dissolved. I felt a wordless transmission of love, directly from his heart to mine. It was a sacred moment beyond the capacity of my rational mind to understand. With the simple power of his gaze, Thầy had awakened my heart to a love that is beyond time and form.

Six years later, I traveled to France to attend a retreat at Plum Village, Thầy's home and practice center. Since that first retreat in Vancouver, I had participated in many others with Thầy. I was now accustomed to how his radiant smile could light up a whole room. I had felt the power of walking together with him and the global Sangha, imprinting peace with every step. I had sat quietly in meditation with him and his beloved community as each mindful breath invited an experience of what he calls interbeing—connectedness with each other and with our precious planet.

This time, as I walked on the familiar paths of Plum Village and sat quietly by the lotus pond, I felt a sense of coming home. My heart felt peaceful and at ease. Yet something was missing: Thầy's physical presence. Our dear teacher had suffered a devastating stroke a few months after the Twenty-One-Day Retreat in 2014, when I had last been here. Although he had recovered somewhat, he was now staying at his monastery in Thailand, where the warmer climate supported his health and healing. The monks and nuns of Plum Village led the retreat I was attending.

Thầy often reminds us to see him in all his different forms. Nonetheless, being at Plum Village without him for the first time I felt a deep sadness in my heart that nothing could fill. Through the practice of mindfulness, I took time to breathe and to be with this feeling of sadness, to see what was beneath the surface. I unearthed a longing to see his beautiful smile, to listen to his gentle words, and to look into his loving eyes just one more time.

Yet I also recognized a deeper longing, not for Thầy's physical form, but for the love and interbeing he points to. Thầy tells us to invite him to walk with us, to breathe with us, and to sit with us during our practice. This has often been my way of staying in touch with him after leaving a retreat and returning home; I decided I would try it right here at Plum Village. I began to imagine I was looking through Thầy's eyes and that he was looking through mine. As I walked around the lotus pond he loved so well, I took off my shoes and invited him to feel the muddy path with my bare feet. I stopped and sat on the wooden bench under the graceful willow tree and gazed across the now fallow pond at the large oriental bell tower that rose out of a terra cotta-colored stone base. Although it was early afternoon, I could almost hear the echo of the Vietnamese nuns chanting the sutras at the beginning and end of each day.

As I walked along, I realized how intimately Thầy knows these paths and these trees. I imagined all the feet from around the world that have walked these sacred paths with him before scattering in all directions like autumn leaves. I imagined the trees recognized Thầy and he recognized them. I wondered if they recognized Thầy in me. I heard the wind in their leaves, and it felt like they were clapping, so happy to see me, so happy to see our beloved teacher in me.

As the retreat continued, the idea came to me that I could be "Thầy in Disguise." I smiled at this thought. Perhaps he would smile too. Instead of leading from up front, he could sit surrounded by the Sangha and just be one of us—really, he already is. At the Day of Mindfulness, the Thầy in me carefully sat down in the third row towards the center of the meditation hall. He watched lovingly as his monastic sons and daughters walked slowly up to the front to chant the sutras. He listened with every cell of his body to both the bell and the harmonious sound of their voices. He smiled. This was a happy moment.

Sister Chan Hoi Nghiem, the Abbess of Plum Village's Lower Hamlet, gave the dharma talk that morning. She looked radiant and confident as she sat in Thầy's place. Knowing the resistance she felt towards the heavy responsibility of becoming Abbess, he would have been proud of her. Now, she seemed to have embraced this new position and to have let go of her doubts. She gave a very deep dharma talk on love, compassion, joy, and equanimity. The Thầy in me felt so much Thầy in her. I felt his joy for his continuation in her and in the Sangha. We all continue Thầy in our own way, whether by walking peacefully, breathing mindfully, sharing kind words, or listening deeply to someone in pain.

After the dharma talk and a short tea break, we gathered by the large bell for walking meditation. This time, Thầy could blend into the middle of the Sangha and watch as his monastic sons and daughters continued to lead us beautifully into the future. The Thầy in me watched as the line of practitioners wound its way through the forest, together becoming a river of peace. I wondered what people would think if they knew Thầy in Disguise was walking beside them, or behind them, or inside of them.

Later, we enjoyed silent lunch in the meditation hall. The monks and men sat in long lines on one side facing the nuns and women sitting on the other side, facing them. Traditionally, Thầy would sit at the far corner in the front row with the elder monks. On this day, however, the Thầy in me was sitting toward the middle of the women's section. From here he could see the earnest faces of his monastic sons, and the beautiful upright backs of his monastic daughters. It was a different view, a different perspective. My heart was full of love and gratitude for being able to see anew through his eyes.

As I sat quietly, I realized some of my sadness had dissolved; Thầy was truly here in me and in the Sangha. I remembered something he had said in one of his last dharma talks at the Twenty-One-Day Retreat in 2014, seeming to look directly at me. I wrote it down in my journal:

> *"Are you caught in longing for something in the future? What are you longing for? You are already what you seek. The wave already knows she is water."*

I had been looking for Thầy outside of myself, but he had been there, inside of me, all along. Reflecting back on that timeless moment spent looking into his eyes just after my mother had died, it occurs to me that my mother, too, is inside of me. The love I always saw in her eyes comes from the same source of love I saw in Thầy's eyes. Her gift of faith was rooted in the Christian tradition, yet it allows me to walk freely in a Buddhist monastery. My expanded faith, encompassing hers and my own, honors and embraces all religions and the love that holds us all.

Perhaps Thầy in Disguise is another name for that timeless, formless love that lies in all of us. Our practice is to simply breathe and to connect to the love we already are.

Vickie MacArthur lives on the traditional lands of the Blackfoot Confederacy in Canada. She is the founder of the Dawning Light Sangha in Lethbridge, Alberta, an interfaith Sangha inspired by Thầy's teachings and practices that is committed to listening deeply to each other and to our world. Vickie was ordained as a minister in the Community of Christ in 2001 and is a lifetime pilgrim on the spiritual path of everyday life. Rooted in Christian, Buddhist, and yogic communities, Vickie is living into her dharma name, Divine Oneness of the Heart, as she aspires to build bridges of understanding between people of different faiths and to create communities beyond the walls of traditional religion. Vickie's memoir, *A Lotus on Fire: How a Buddhist Monk Ignited the Love in My Heart,* is a story of awakening to the love beyond culture and religion that combines the calm of the Zen mind with the passion of the Christian mystic's heart.

The Whole Universe in an Apple

by Huy Minh Tran

I WAS SIX YEARS OLD when the communists took control of Vietnam in 1975. In my short lifetime I had known only war, but life after the war was no better. As deputy general manager of the Reserve Bank, my father was considered antagonistic to the new regime; he was sent to a "re-education camp," in reality a forced labor camp where South Vietnamese men were detained in harsh living conditions for years. The communists stole our livelihood, our house, our car, our pets, and, worst of all, my beloved brother's life. For many years afterward, I had recurrent dreams of my brother being swept out to sea and a voice from above asking whether I would like to die in his place. I always said "yes" and always woke up sobbing.

Constantly persecuted by the new government, my parents realized that we would be better off sinking to the bottom of the ocean than trying to live in that society. We escaped Vietnam on a twenty-four-meter longboat; 474 people sat upright for three days until we shipwrecked in Malaysia. Running back and forth on a dark beach, desperately trying to find my parents and two sisters, I feared

I had lost everything. Eventually we found each other; hugging tightly with only the shirts on our backs, we felt like the happiest family on earth.

At the refugee camp in Malaysia we lacked clean water, basic supplies, and adequate food. We slept on beds made from branches that poked into our backs, and Mum stayed up all night fanning mosquitoes away. My parents sold their wedding rings to buy some necessities, and with a little of the remaining money, they bought apples for my sisters and me. Amidst such hardship, that apple was the most beautiful thing I had ever tasted. I innocently asked Dad if he could please buy me another one when he had more money; I thought I could eat a million apples and never get bored of them. Although the reality that he had nothing left to sell stung him, my dad smiled, stroked my head, and promised that one day he would buy me lots of apples.

Staying true to his word, when we finally made it to Australia my parents kept buying apples—so many that after about a thousand of them, I could not eat another apple for thirty years.

My parents worked tirelessly to provide for us three children. At the same time, they dedicated their lives to contributing to society and performing charity to help others. I understood my parents' love and care and the sacrifices they made, so I worked hard at school to make them happy. Determined to please my parents, in year five I completed a year's worth of a math workbook in two weeks.

When I was seventeen, Thích Nhất Hạnh came to Australia. "A *bodhisattva*!" my parents exclaimed. To have a visit from such a respected teacher from our own culture and home country, a dedicated traveler on the path of mindfulness, sent a wave of excitement through our community. Everyone described Thầy as the father of mindfulness practice in the Western world.

My parents, my two sisters, and I attended his public talk at Phap Bao Pagoda. Thầy's message was simple: There is no way to happiness; happiness is the way. With that foundational concept, my parents became two of the original members of the Lotus Bud Sangha in Sydney and began attending retreats at Plum Village to deepen their practice. Dad received the dharma name Chân Viên Âm, "perfect speech," and Mum, Chân Liên Hương, "lotus fragrance."

Thầy's impact on my parents was deep and lasting. Growing up in their mindful atmosphere inspired me to study medicine and become a general practitioner in order to help as many people as possible. However, as an adult, I was not part of a Sangha and did not practice regularly. When Dad passed away in 2012 and Mum in 2014, I suffered greatly. At forty-five years of age I felt like that lost refugee boy again, frantically searching the beach in Malaysia, alone and afraid that everything was lost. Each thing I saw brought back memories of my beloved parents, and I cried often. At home I hid in the bathroom to cry so that I would not transfer the negative energy to my wife and sons. Because I had studied Thầy's teachings, I knew about impermanence, the idea that change is happening to everything and everyone, all the time. I knew that suffering is fleeting, that we all experience it, and that it is not necessarily bad—it can bring healing and transformation. Even so, knowing was not true understanding; I could not yet fully accept my parents' death.

Fortunately, two very wise and dear friends of my parents, uncle Chân Đạo Hành and aunty Chân Tuệ Hương, asked me a startling question: "Would you like to see your parents again?" The way, they explained, was to come back to mindfulness. They invited me to join them at Bankstown Mindfulness Practice Centre, where we meditated and listened to Thầy's teachings. With daily practice, I realized that mindfulness is not something I need to set aside time for in my busy life. It is an integrated part, present in every moment. Each mindful breath, each mindful step, and each compassionate thought, speech, or action gives me joy, peace, and happiness. I invite Thầy and my parents to practice mindfulness alongside me in each moment.

In October 2018, our Sangha visited Plum Village, Thailand, and we were blessed with the opportunity to meet Thầy. There we were, my wife Trâm and me, bowing to Thầy. But in reality, it was not just the two of us. I invited my father and my mother inside of me to visit Plum Village Thailand too. They had not been there before, and I invited them to meet Thầy; it had been many years since they had last been with him. I physically felt the presence of my parents inside me; father, mother, and son bowed as one in gratitude, and as Thầy gently smiled and bowed back, we experienced ultimate peace and happiness.

Thầy teaches that mindfulness is a practice, an active engagement, and not just a theory or a philosophy. Through this practice, I found my parents again. They are always present, in every cell in my body. Their loving thoughts and speech, their compassionate actions, are always present in my mind and manifested in my actions.

Breathing in, I feel calm and peaceful for my dad.
Breathing out, I smile happily for my mum.

I know now that meditation is not a practice of hoping for some positive outcome in the future. I meditate because I enjoy the peace, happiness, and endless wonders of the present moment. This frees me from being imprisoned by the past or worrying about the future.

I breathe with my dad's lungs.
I smile with my mum's lips.
I walk in meditation with my brother's legs.

I no longer cry or have sad dreams about losing my beloved parents and brother. Before tears start to flow, Thầy reminds me I am their continuation and we all feel ultimate peace and happiness together, here and now. Apples are again a special part of my life. I feel my parents' love, caring, and compassion in each bite; I can touch the whole universe in one apple.

Huy Minh Tran lives in Australia and practices with the Bankstown Mindfulness Practice Centre in Sydney. He views his dharma name, Wisdom of Radiant Light, Minh Quang, as given not just to him, but also to everyone and everything around him in this universe, because there is so much to learn. His parents and oldest brother have passed away, and he has two older sisters, a wife, and two sons. He is a doctor who appreciates his Sangha for helping him create beautiful moments of peace and happiness.

PART 3

Coming Home
to Ourselves

Just One Look

by Kaira Jewel Lingo

IN 2003, I TRAVELED WITH Thích Nhất Hạnh and several hundred monastic and lay students to China to offer retreats, public talks, and Days of Mindfulness in different parts of the country. At that time, I was a nun in Thầy's community. Like all teaching tours with him, this one was more like a pilgrimage—many inner and outer blessings and challenges called forth the best in us, while helping us to compassionately recognize and befriend the worst in us.

At some point on the trip, I started feeling very bad about myself. For several days I experienced gnawing self-doubt, fueled by self-judgment and aversion to who I felt I was and what was going on inside me: the kind of self-absorbed thinking that narrows your mind and cuts you off from others, heavy emotions so consuming and persuasive you cannot connect with or be open to other realities.

That morning, we were en route from one city to another, and I remember boarding the bus full of misery, feeling utterly dejected and desperate. Thầy was sitting in the front row, as he always did, to make sure the driver stayed awake and that we would all be safe. As I got to the top step, I lifted my gaze and our eyes met. Thầy was looking at me most intently, with a compassion and love so huge I felt it physically. A palpable energy of affirmation, care, and deep understanding of my pain penetrated my body and mind. I had never seen that depth of kindness in someone's eyes before, and especially never directed at me. As if a great being or Buddha were looking at me through a magnifying glass of unconditional love, the look was so focused that it burned away attachment to my story and removed the deluded tendrils and seductive hooks keeping me bound up in the little picture, the small self. It was a moment of grace, and it took my breath away.

Though I had to continue moving past Thầy to take my seat, inside I had stopped completely. I was changed. Thầy's brief look opened up a moment of timelessness in the midst of the pressures of worldly time, and it created a moment of well-being and wholeness in the midst of intense suffering and brokenness. Thầy's look taught me that awakening is possible in every moment, even if it is a tiny waking up to the reality of this moment, where innate goodness and worthiness can always be affirmed.

His look kindled a deep desire to be able to look at other people in that way myself, with boundless compassion and love that can wordlessly relieve suffering and inspire great confidence and joy.

I think back to the many things Thầy might have been preoccupied with in that moment, for the trips to China were especially challenging ones. We were a Buddhist delegation in a communist country that was at times welcoming, at times ambiguous, and at times suspicious of our presence. Thầy was guiding not just several hundred lay and monastic followers but digging deep into his own vast knowledge and experience to be able to offer culturally appropriate teachings to thousands of Chinese people. At the same time, he was gently, and sometimes not so gently, encouraging them to move beyond narrow views and reclaim their powerful ancestral wisdom. He had his own health and safety to be concerned about, as well as that of all of us who accompanied him. And yet, right in the midst of it, he was free from all of that: free enough to see me clearly, free enough to care about me, and free enough to zap me with incredible peace and freedom.

Kaira Jewel Lingo lives on Long Island, New York and comes from a family with deep roots with Thích Nhất Hạnh. She practices with the Buddhist Christian Community of Meditation and Action online and with the Black, Indigenous, and People of Color Meditation Sangha, online through the Garrison Institute. Kaira Jewel was ordained as a novice nun with Thích Nhất Hạnh in 1999 and given the name True Adornment with Jewel. At first, she felt uncomfortable with the name Jewel, thinking it seemed flashy, until another nun shared that a jewel, such as a diamond, is formed when intense pressure creates a substance that is very stable and strong. Kaira Jewel now views her dharma name as inspiration to be useful and to help manifest what is needed. She is the author of *We Were Made for These Times: Ten Lessons on Moving through Change, Loss and Disruption,* and she edited *Planting Seeds: Practicing Mindfulness with Children,* by Thích Nhất Hạnh.

Owning My Voice

by Trish Thompson

THE EARLY AFTERNOON SUN INVITES me to lie down and relax in its warmth. After all, I have nowhere to go and nothing to do on this cold day on the coast of Maine, where I've retreated for a year of solitude. I've taken refuge in this environment, alien to a southerner; the harsh winters invite and support deep reflection.

My cottage sits on a hillside at the end of a narrow, rough driveway, hidden from the eyes of those passing on the road that runs along the cove 100 yards below. I've made no friends in the fishing village, nor have I tried. There will be no unexpected visitors, and for this I am grateful. I've wanted and badly needed this alone time.

Half awake, half asleep, I drift into a state of total relaxation in the warm sun on my glassed-in porch. Suddenly, I hear a voice in my head.

"Mamie, shut up! You talk too much!" The voice belongs to my father. He directs his words at my mother.

Startled, my eyes pop open. I am totally alert. His voice rings in my ears, a voice I haven't heard for more than forty years.

I am a child again. I am in the room watching them, as I often did. Once again, they are arguing. My mother is talking, talking, saying terrible things about my father, about his family, about his inability to stand up for himself against his father, about his choice of friends. On and on, she vents her anger.

My father, as usual, is not looking at her, not responding. This time, he refuses to engage. Though sometimes, he did. Afterwards, we would say, "Daddy lost his temper," our way of understanding his rage and his fists. Tears come as I remember the suffering of my mother and father and of my child self, Little Trish.

My thoughts go to my own two marriages. The first one, between two very young people with no idea how to work with the challenges that would eventually overwhelm them, produced three children. After nineteen years, it ended in an extremely painful divorce.

Now the second marriage, of almost as many years, is also ending.

Both husbands said I talked too much. "You always have something to say. You talk too much. No one wants to hear what you have to say. Why don't you just shut up?"

I reflect on the years I suffered from the anxiety of trying to be myself while appeasing the man in my life. I developed a keen awareness and sensitivity toward how much I said and how long I took to say it. I became hyper-conscious of not infringing on another's time. Fear of talking too much affected the professional life I eventually created for myself. A watch or a clock was always in view when I gave a presentation. I rehearsed my presentations. No spontaneity for me; I stuck with the script!

Now, at age sixty, "conditions had become sufficient," as the Buddha would say, to reveal the root cause of my inability to trust my voice. My path of awakening had included psychotherapy, with a focus on healing the inner child. I had moved through various spiritual practices and communities—the Course in Miracles, shamanism, Native American spirituality, Tibetan Buddhism. All had been important to me. Eventually, I found my way to a retreat at Plum Village, Thích Nhất Hạnh's practice center in France. In a silent, profoundly intense moment of recognition, I immediately knew I had met my teacher.

Following that encounter with Thầy, I made a deeper commitment to practice mindfulness throughout each day and to be happy to live fully in the present moment. With the practice and support of my teachers and Sangha, I slowly learned to love myself. As my practice became more solid, my capacity to extend that love to others and my devotion to developing boundless compassion grew.

Fast-forward from Maine 2001 to Hanoi, Vietnam, 2007. Thầy has returned to his home country for his second teaching tour, bringing an international Sangha with him, as he had done in 2005. That historic occasion in 2005, the Joyfully Together three-month teaching tour, was his first visit to his home country after thirty-nine years in exile. Accompanying Thầy and the Sangha in 2005, I fell in love with the people and chose to stay in Vietnam, surprising friends, family, and even myself!

During the winter retreat at Plum Village after that 2005 tour, Thầy asked me to organize two evenings for his second visit to Hanoi. He would give public talks in English. What an honor and great happiness to have an opportunity to be of service to my teacher and Sangha! There was, however, one small challenge in fulfilling Thầy's request. The Community of Mindful Living, which I had founded in Hanoi, was not registered with the government; we did not formally exist. The wonderful volunteer organization, Friends of Vietnam Heritage, rescued us, providing the needed credentials for booking a hotel and holding a public, high-profile function. We decided that John, a local businessman and the organization's long-time chairman, would introduce Thầy at the first talk.

The first venue was the Melia Hotel. As expected, the ballroom was full. We had prepared a small waiting room for Thầy and his attendants, stocking it with water, tea, and copies of the flyer we had distributed throughout the city. Just before the evening began, I was summoned to meet with Thầy. He sweetly asked, "Please tell me, dear Trish, who am I talking to this evening?" I listed the categories of people and some of the individuals who had registered: students, foreign business people, Vietnamese intellectuals, several ambassadors, and so on. He nodded, approvingly I thought, and then asked, "And what am I talking about?" I gave him the evening's title, the one on the flyer.

Right on time, John appeared and escorted Thầy to the dais. He then gave a brief speech welcoming the Zen master to Hanoi.

Two weeks later, we were at the Sheraton for the second scheduled evening, and I was to introduce Thầy. Eight hundred people filled the ballroom. I had tried to prepare a few words of welcome and introduction, but my mind had been too full of the event planning details. I had been unable to concentrate on writing a speech. Now it was show time, and my mind was empty.

Standing in the hotel corridor waiting for Thầy and Sr. Chan Khong to emerge from the waiting room, I felt a curious mixture of anticipation and calmness. The door opened, and there they were, my two beloved teachers. After smiles and bows, Thầy asked, "Now who am I talking to tonight?" I told him. He nodded gently. "And what am I talking about?" I gave him the title, "Peace in Oneself, Peace in the World."

And then, "You know that man who introduced me at the Melia Hotel?"

Sister Chan Khong, whose memory for names and people is unmatched, quickly interjected, "John."

Thầy continued, "Yes, John. He didn't have much to say. Maybe you can talk more."

I stared at him for one tiny second before bursting into laughter. "Oh, Thầy, I can talk!"

And Thầy, that remarkable Zen master who knows his disciples so well, also laughed as he used the back of his hand to playfully hit my forearm.

We walked into the ballroom together, and I calmly introduced my beloved teacher to a packed room. No watch or clock was necessary. I spoke until I was finished. I looked at the Zen master. He looked at me. The communication was perfect.

Trish Thompson, whose dharma name is True Concentration on Peace, lives in Vietnam, where she is the founder and managing director of the Loving Work Foundation, which she created to improve the lives of children and families. A lay dharma teacher, Trish has made her home in Vietnam since 2005, building community, leading mindfulness retreats for international friends, and engaging in various humanitarian projects. In addition, she happily supports Joyful Garden Sangha in Singapore and the practice of Sangha members throughout Southeast Asia. Trish, originally from Charleston, South Carolina, is a member of the Plum Blossom and Cedar Society, which offers stable, long-term funding support for the Plum Village community.

So Much in a Cup of Tea

by Paz Perlman

I DID NOT WANT A teacher or a Sangha. Painful experiences with former teachers in various Buddhist traditions had taught me that practicing alone, without a guide or a community of practice, was my safest choice. In fact, I had been happily meditating daily on my own for quite some time.

By chance I picked up Thích Nhất Hạnh's book, *Peace is Every Step,* as I headed out the door for a vacation in France. I do not remember how long it had been on my bookshelf; for some reason, I had never opened it.

During that vacation I opened the book and could not put it down. As soon as I finished, I started reading it all over again, and again. I was captivated by the simplicity and depth of Thầy's teachings. Unlike other Buddhist writers, who can be intellectual and conceptual, Thầy made the teachings accessible and practical.

Soon afterwards, when I heard that Thầy was holding a retreat where I lived in the Netherlands, it was clear that I needed to go. I wanted to directly experience his way of teaching and practicing.

It was not what I expected. In fact, I found it very strange.

When I had studied in the Japanese Zen tradition, we sat in silence for eight hours at a stretch, looking at a wall. In the Tibetan tradition that I practiced later, we focused on ceremonies and chanting mantras. Thầy's retreat included guided meditations, singing what seemed like simple children's songs, and dharma sharing groups that incorporated a mix of Buddhism and Western psychology. It was a starkly different experience from what I knew of Zen.

To cap it all off, Sister Chan Khong, who had spent her life working side by side with Thầy to create the Plum Village tradition, started singing lullabies during the total relaxation session one day after lunch. On one level, I was touched by her innocence and child-like lack of inhibition; on another, I was confronted with my own self-consciousness, and I felt uncomfortable and disoriented. I was convinced I would never come back!

Yet I had been deeply impressed by Thầy's talk preceding the retreat and by his immense presence during the retreat's dharma talks. Despite my surface concerns, something deeper in me recognized I had met a great teacher. When I moved shortly afterwards to the United Kingdom and saw that Thầy was offering a retreat at Nottingham University, I felt called to try again. I was so moved by the end that I committed to the Five Mindfulness Trainings, a framework that guides us to create more happiness for ourselves and the world around us.

My partner Jo, a journalist at *The Guardian*, joined me at that retreat and interviewed Thầy. Jo felt an instant connection with him, and Thầy invited us to visit Plum Village, his community in France.

We took him up on his offer and traveled to Plum Village later that year to join the winter retreat. Just a few months before, we had gotten married in a civil ceremony in the UK, but at Plum Village we felt an urge to add a spiritual dimension to that commitment. We asked Thầy for permission to be married in the monastery, and he agreed.

The beautiful and moving ceremony, which included offering incense and the practice of Touching the Earth, was conducted by Sister Chan Khong. Also present were a number of monastics and lay practitioners seated in rows of silent support, facing each other. Jo and I had written our own vows, which we read aloud during the ceremony in front of the Sangha. The atmosphere was both loving and intimate. We were now family, and the Sangha would always be there to support us, Sister Chan Khong said as she presented us with a marriage certificate.

The next day, Thầy invited us to have tea with him. I remember my heart beating fast and strong as we entered his room and looked upon a scene that could have been thousands of years old: a small room with the most warm and cozy atmosphere and Thầy sitting on a hammock with his back to us in the middle of it, surrounded by his attendants. We sat drinking tea in silence, and I felt I was sitting next to a great river. When I looked into Thầy's eyes, it felt like I was looking simultaneously into emptiness and great tenderness.

He asked us a simple question: How had our experience staying in Plum Village been? While there were many things I could have said about my great happiness during the previous two weeks, I was surprised by what came out of my mouth. In answer, I told Thầy that I felt truly safe, even as the only woman in Upper Hamlet among nearly 200 monks and male lay practitioners. This was pleasantly new to me after having experienced, both in my childhood and in the practice centers of other traditions, inappropriate behavior from men towards me.

Thầy sat quietly and did not respond to what I had said. I immediately went into feelings of insecurity, worrying I had said something of no consequence. We sat with Thầy for quite some time, and it was joyful in many ways, yet when we left him, I felt disappointed in myself. Had I missed a golden opportunity to use my time well with one of the greatest living spiritual masters?

I was unable to let go of this self-doubt until many months later, when a monastic who came to stay with us brought a CD of the Christmas dharma talk Thầy had given soon after we had visited Plum Village. In the talk, Thầy said, "In Plum Village, every time you hear the bell, you stop thinking, you stop talking, you stop doing things. You pay attention to your in-breath as you breathe in and you say, 'I listen, I listen. This wonderful sound brings me back to my true home.' My true home is inside. My true home is in the here and the now.

"Practicing going home is what we do all day long, because we are only comfortable in our true home. Our true home is available, and we can go home every moment. Our home should be safe, intimate, and cozy, and it is we who make it that way.

"Last week I had tea with a couple who came from the United Kingdom. They spent two weeks in Plum Village, with the monks in the Upper Hamlet. The lady said, 'It's strange. It's the first time I've lived in a place with hundreds of men and no women, and I feel very safe in the Upper Hamlet. I have never felt safe like that.'

"In the Upper Hamlet she was the only woman, and she felt very safe. And if she feels safe, the place is her home, because home should provide that kind of safety. Are you a safe place for him or for her? Do you have enough stability, strength, protection for the one you love?"

When I heard this, all my suffering dissolved and I understood very deeply Thầy's teaching about true home. I understood the importance of acknowledging my own suffering around feeling safe. In that moment I let go, and everything fell into place. I recognized that Thầy, by being a safe space himself, has created a safe space for others and for me.

Paz Perlman is originally from Israel and now lives in France, about a ten-minute walk from Plum Village, where she practices regularly. She was ordained into the Order of Interbeing in 2017 and given the name True Manifestation of Compassion. Noting the combination of the three words—true, manifestation, and compassion—she believes that compassion is not a quality she needs to work hard for; rather, it depends on her waiting for the right conditions to manifest truly. Her name reminds her to stay open. Paz is an artist who expresses her practice of healing and transformation through her works of art.

My Kumbaya Moment

by Susan Patrice Garofalo

THE RELIGIOUS TRADITION MY PARENTS passed to me at birth was presented like an impossibly perfect gift box, beribboned and adorned, too fancy to be opened, too pretty to be disturbed, too tidy to be explored. It sat admired on a shelf of honor until it finally collected enough dust and dents to justify my ripping through the once-glossy wrappings. Inside, I found a splendid garment that proclaimed my membership in a belief system that surpassed all others.

Well into my adult years, I wore the glory of my family's religious tradition with pious pride, cloaking myself in a costume I fiercely wanted to fit into. Wrapped in its glittery splendor, I felt I knew God so well I could explain him to anyone; if called upon, I could even have offered a visual aid: an elaborate rendering of the Trinity, complete with diagrams, detailed enlargements, and scripture captions.

For all my insistence and performance, though, I didn't actually feel God, and I found myself in the habit of echoing the refrain of a ubiquitous folk anthem. Crying out for his presence, I would plead, "Kumbaya!"

Kumbaya, my Lord! Kumbaya!

This Gullah spiritual, which rose from the hearts of enslaved people yearning for God to "come by here," became my mantra for decades as I pulled my garment tighter year after year. My Catholic faith required that I identify first and foremost as a sinner, but it extended the accommodation that my sins could be forgiven if I confessed them secretly to a man seated behind a screened partition in a dark, closet-like chamber. I, in turn, accepted that I was separate from God and that my value as a human being required me to rely on his earthly surrogates. I accepted the Catholic Church's demand that we adhere to the commandments delivered to Moses on Mount Sinai but also to the many wide-ranging decrees from the Vatican. I was encouraged by the church's promise that, worst-case scenario, if I managed to bury myself under a lifetime of mortal sins, I could be saved from hell by crying out at the moment of my death. Like the thief crucified next to Jesus. "Kumbaya, my Lord!"

Similarly, the parish priest who molested me during my teen years, a time when I aspired to serve the Lord as a nun, could also be saved—an irony that I was oblivious to. I had no idea that I had entombed that priest's abuse in an abyss of dissociation so complete it took me thirty years to wake up from my trance. Seated at the kitchen table in the winter of 2002, I "came to" staring into the cold, congealed, half-eaten egg I had soft boiled for breakfast hours before. Startled and then panicked, I was completely unable to account for those lost hours until I reread the headline in the New York Times on the table in front of me, "Boston Priests' Sex-Abuse Scandal Has Ripple Effect."

By 2002, years of trying to metabolize the religious teachings I consumed had accustomed my liver to daily onslaughts of alcohol. Nothing could fill the void or relieve my pain. For all my longing for a true connection with God, the central, most tender, most fertile piece of me was untouched, untended, and barren.

Kumbaya!

Trying to make sense of my life and my spirituality—to reconcile what was visible for all to see with what happened in secret—was like trying to grab and reconnect splintered objects while spinning in the heart of a tornado. Trapped in a world I saw as black and white, where everything had to be either perfect or ruined, there was no room for me, who was neither. So I found myself edging toward the black, groping for a way out, until an intervention landed me in the office of a therapist familiar with the teachings of Thích Nhất Hạnh.

At his suggestion, I leafed through the opening pages of *The Miracle of Mindfulness*, and color and texture began to bleed into my life. Bit by bit, I felt some spaciousness, some solidity, as my own breath gradually brought vibrance and vitality into my being. Healing, health, even a future became possible.

Thầy's formula for navigating this planet didn't conjure the slightest wisp of the hocus-pocus I was accustomed to at mass or sacraments. There were no transubstantiations to strain to witness, no magical prayer formulas offered as penance to remove my sins, my guilt, or my shame. I found comfort in the unapologetic common sense and scientific clarity of Thầy's Buddhist teachings.

Thầy's words threaded through me as precious, glimmering strands knitting the gaps that most needed to be filled. My new cloak was being woven from within.

As Thầy's teachings put my world into sharper focus and revealed my true original goodness, I started seeing how threadbare my life-worn religious uniform had become. Over time, I started squirming out of it, this garment now splitting at the seams to make space for growth, inclusion, self-love, and, quite literally, breath.

Therapy, rehab, and twelve-step programs played important parts in my recovery, but meditation was the gateway to understanding and transformation. I relished Thầy's gentle guidance to recognize, follow, and enjoy my in-breath and my out-breath. If I became aware of a thought, he encouraged me to notice it, acknowledge my thinking, and let it go, returning my focus to my breath.

One day, while sitting with my breath, following it through my body, I became aware of an all-too-familiar thought: *Kumbaya!*

As Thầy suggests, I said "hello" to that call. I recognized it as the utterance that involuntarily springs from my lips during times of unease and apprehension, or during memories of helplessness and trauma. The utterance whispered in subways, churches, and conference rooms—the one smothered in the darkness of my bedroom at night. I acknowledged that I was once again beseeching God to come by me. And then, as Thầy instructs, I remained as calm and steady as a blue sky and let the cloud of my thought drift out of sight.

Returning to my breath, I knew I was breathing in and I knew I was breathing out. A few moments later, I realized something had bubbled up from my soul. Written on the back of my eyelids was a single word: "Here."

In that moment, everything about me shifted toward transformation. It registered undeniably, on a cellular level. I was dumbstruck by the realization that I had spent my whole life desperately begging God to come to me when all along God, as the Ultimate, the infinite realm beyond birth and death, had never been farther away than my own breath. There was no longer a need to reach outside myself.

In that moment, I touched God in my own Buddha nature, as surely as my fingers clasped each other in my lap. In that moment, I entered fully into the process of abandoning all notions of being a victim, of relying on God's mercy, or of depending on forgiveness dispensed by an interpreter in pompous ritual. I started to see that, in every second of every day, I was accountable for my choices in speech and thought and action. I saw that crying out for forgiveness at the moment of my death would do nothing to arrest any harm I might have inflicted on my loved ones, harm that would ripple out into the universe, even past my lifetime. From that moment on, I sought to heal the past and to create my future in the present.

Susan Patrice Garofalo lives in the United States and practices with several Sanghas including the Practice Community of Franklin Lakes, New Jersey, and Blue Cliff Monastery in New York. She says her dharma name, Compassionate Service of the Heart, is perfect for her, as service brings her great joy. Susan is a professional writer and ghostwriter for legislators and political candidates active in the areas of social justice and criminal justice reform. She has written children's books and is currently working on a memoir.

There Is Something in His Gaze

by Celia Landman

THE FIRST TIME I ENCOUNTERED nine hundred people at once was at a Who concert, and it didn't go well. We were at Boston Garden, a large music and sports arena, and when fights broke out, I was pulled along by the surge of the jostling, muscular crowd. I remember armoring myself with an angry toughness, stiffening to make my body as solid as I could to guard myself from being squeezed or knocked over. It was an ordeal to get out of the venue and a relief to feel the cool air again.

Twenty years later, I wondered how I would feel among nine hundred people at a Buddhist retreat. Surely that would be different, but I still didn't know if I'd feel safe when I arrived at Blue Cliff Monastery, a retreat center in upstate New York. Despite my fears of pushing and shoving, long bathroom lines, lack of food and courtesy, I wanted to know what it was like to be in the presence of Thích Nhất Hạnh.

As a child of both Jewish and Catholic parents, I often say I was raised with "the best of both guilts." In the Western world, I encountered models of conditional love and worth. If I were a good enough student, child, professional, or contributing member of the community, I would earn a place. If I stepped outside expectations, even though they were often unexpressed, I would find censure and blame. There was a clear message that my value was based on what I did, not who I was. In the Buddhist and Plum Village teaching, I was instructed to see my strength and value and to seek healing through connecting with my ancestors. The idea of including my ancestors as allies was new for me and offered a different way of seeing myself: not as a small, separate being, needing to keep up standards, but as a continuation. Knowing I was part of a lineage helped me see that I had a right to be here on this Earth—I was part of nature just as much as the trees, the stones, and the sky.

Up until that point, my relationship with organized religion had been tentative. It seemed to me that all religious groups asked me what I could give to them, how I could fit into their model. Thầy and the Buddha asked, "How is this teaching for you? What is your experience?" With Buddhism, there was no expectation of compliance, in contrast to what I had grown up with, nor was there the message that some fundamental badness in me needed repair before I was worthy of belonging.

For the first dharma talk of the retreat, I sat a few rows from the front. The air in the large hall was humid. There was the scratchy sound of nylon rain jackets being folded and stowed as people positioned themselves on cushions and in chairs, taking out water bottles and notebooks in preparation for the dharma talk. At the sound of a bell, we all stood to welcome Thầy. I faced the long center aisle, waiting for him to enter. A few feet from where I stood, the side door opened, and I turned quickly to see a small man about my height step into the hall. He wore a floor-length brown robe, and his attendants, taller but with the same robes and shaved heads, walked in behind him.

He stopped by the door and looked around the room. His eyes met mine with a calm stillness. He was not smiling, and his face could have belonged to someone very young or very old, one of those ageless faces that retained a child's tenderness and vulnerability. His expression was not childish but somewhere between solemn and soft as he walked with mindful steps into the Great Togetherness Hall.

When Thầy looked at the large crowd, I had the distinct feeling he saw me. In that moment of being seen, I experienced a sense of being known, understood, and accepted. It was as if he knew the very worst thing I had done in my life, and the most terrible secrets of this human crowd, but held no judgment, no fear or disgust—only understanding. My eyes teared up as he held me in this field of compassion. I was seen and known as I was. Held by his gaze, I felt welcomed and forgiven.

After the talk, the Sangha walked with Thầy up a grassy hill, not steep, but for someone with difficulty balancing, it was a mountain. The group moved in the direction of Sister Chan Khong's hut and then stopped. I walked holding the arm of my dear friend Judith, and we went slowly, her with her cane, me holding her arm to steady her body. We moved together, taking small steps to avoid the rocks and uneven ground, and were the last to reach the top of the hill, far behind the rest of the Sangha. Arriving, we saw the wide circle of folks gathered around Thầy, who was drinking from a small cup of tea. He lowered his teacup and watched as we walked slowly towards him with cane and arms linked. His eyes held us and stayed upon us: the last ones, climbing slowly, Judith tentative with vertigo and my steps trimmed to match hers.

Thầy's eyes reflected a softness and willingness to wait for us as if there was no hurry in all the world. In that wide-open space where time didn't matter, I felt that we truly did. We were held in his care. Irrepressible tears welled up again as I saw myself through Thầy's eyes and could imagine I was somehow worthy. Holy. I was absolved of all my mistakes, my unkind words, the ways I was critical of myself and others, and seen, despite my anger and fears and the flaws and imperfections that needed defending, for the goodness in me. Somehow, I was loved in his eyes, exactly as I was.

There is a word, *drishti*, in the Hindi language. It speaks of the importance of seeing and being seen by a holy person. Drishti aids spiritual development and acknowledges the importance of this shared gaze. It is the felt presence, the energy of mindfulness, that Thầy transmitted to me that day.

When I returned home from the retreat, I told my mother, "I think that is what it was like to see Jesus. There's something in his gaze. Something about being seen." People flocked to Jesus for something beyond the words of biblical scriptures, something connected to a love bigger than a country or an ideology. Although I couldn't access that experience of love through the Christian scripture, like my mother did, that was what I sensed. This all-encompassing love became a possibility when I saw it alive in the Sangha. I couldn't express what happened; it was the feeling of being safe, and my heart knew it when it happened. I had received a teaching about love, transmitted without words. As a person who grew up learning that making mistakes meant danger and shame, this love pierced through forty-four years of protective armor. I didn't need to be right or flawless to be safe in the world. I was good enough, just as I was.

In Thầy's gaze was the seed of learning to love myself with the same acceptance, understanding, and forgiveness that he had given me. The seed of compassion that Thầy watered in me that day has grown from a small dry kernel into an abundant flower. He taught me to gaze at myself with gentle eyes of acceptance. I had never before been held that way, in the light of non-judgment.

Afterwards, I felt more confidence and trust in the path of practice. I started to volunteer to facilitate Sangha meetings and used the practice of dharma sharing, the place of deep listening and mindful speech, to safely share my journey of healing my heart. When I was listened to in the Sangha, without people trying to fix me or speed up my process, I encountered the lesson of acceptance and self-compassion again and again.

Like slow drops of water against rock, little by little, this acceptance softened my fear and defensiveness. The seeds of confidence and trust were nourished by true friends in the Sangha who supported me and by my dharma teacher, Joanne Friday, who saw me as good and loveable. I learned to speak from my heart and found the willingness to be vulnerable. I began to see myself as part of this interconnected life and to see that my birthright was goodness. When I could believe that, I could see the love I longed for was all around me. What kept it away were the barriers I had built against it.

Today, I work with teens in rehab who've learned to run from their feelings and don't know how to feel safe or at peace. They have never heard that they are connected to their ancestors, that they are part of the Earth, or that their legacy is solidity and strength. They don't believe that they are enough. The seeds of craving and despair are strong in their lives. I remind them of their true heritage, remind them that they are woven into the fabric of the universe, each one valuable and deserving of a beautiful life. I water their seeds of belonging and self-compassion. I "see them," and I tell them that they are good at their core—and yes, I answer, I am sure.

Celia Landman lives in the United States and practices with the Earth Holders Sangha in Litchfield, Connecticut. Her dharma name, Deep Illumination of the Heart, is an acknowledgment of the light in her heart when she sees her own goodness and the goodness of others. It takes mindfulness to maintain awareness that, even if outward actions appear harmful, there is always light. Celia has a master's degree in Mindfulness Studies from Lesley University and is a mother and a partner. Her greatest aspiration is to help others recognize their true nature of love and ability. Protecting young people and all life is what gets her out of bed in the morning, and poetry brings her to life. Her book, *When the Whole World Tips: Parenting through Crisis with Mindfulness and Balance,* is forthcoming from Parallax Press..

Suddenly I Realize
I Need Nothing Else

by Eevi Beck

WHEN MY HUSBAND, SVEIN, AND I first got together, we knew within five days, and without having talked about it, that we wanted to marry at Plum Village in France. Svein was a meditation teacher in Thích Nhất Hạnh's tradition, and Plum Village is its international core community. Our dear families thought us crazy to marry so soon, and they were partly right. My attraction to Svein was fueled by a strong sense of coming home during an introductory meditation course he had taught in our native Norway. Because of his gentle wisdom during that course, I assumed our relationship would be easy. Yet right from the start, Svein urged me to befriend my pain and to transform my excruciating self-critique. This went against all I had learned about how to behave! He said the homecoming I had experienced in that meditation course had been coming home to myself. I didn't get it.

Within a year of meeting, Svein and I did get married, both in a Christian church in Norway and at Plum Village. The Plum Village ceremony had deep spiritual significance but no legal status. The core of the ceremony was Thầy's transmission of the Five Awarenesses for Couples. This practice consists of reading and talking about these five statements together each month:

- ◎ We are aware that all previous generations of ancestors and all future generations are in us.

- ◎ We are aware of the expectations that our ancestors, our children, and their children have of us.

- ◎ We are aware that our peace, joy, freedom, and harmony are the peace, joy, freedom, and harmony of our ancestors, our children, and their children.

- ◎ We are aware that understanding is the foundation of love.

- ◎ We are aware that arguing and blaming never helps but creates a wider gap between us. Only trust and love can help us change and grow.

The day before the wedding, we had tea with Thầy. I was astounded at his gentle simplicity and kindness. And when he sipped his tea, he did nothing else. I had already met the teachings on mindfully drinking tea, yet experiencing the depth of Thầy's enjoyment had me transfixed beyond words. Was it really possible? So much time for such a simple act. And what deep peace I felt just being next to him! I had not known that a longing for such peace existed inside of me, let alone that drinking a cup of tea could touch it. Coming home to myself, indeed!

During our meeting with Thầy, Svein asked me to share a poem I had written to express an insight I had during a dharma talk a few days earlier:

> Sister Annabel's words flow like clear water over pebbles
> Svein is inviting the bell with deep love
> The gentle brother next to me lets me benefit from his fan
> And suddenly I realize: I need nothing else

After listening to the poem, Thầy said a few kind words about it, and I thought it compassionate of him to offer a beginner such politeness. I had also prepared a question for Thầy about stress at work. He gently said that my poem had the answer—have no ambition. He emphasized: no ambition at all.

I struggled with self-centered shyness, wondering, How could *my* poem carry such weight? But Svein was freer, and he asked Thầy, "What about ambition to share the teachings?" Thầy's answer was stern, leaving no doubt that the poem's insight was enough.

For days, weeks, and months after our meeting with Thầy, Svein practiced to digest the message that even sharing the Buddha's teachings should not become an ambition. Do it, but without clinging to an outcome. Meanwhile, I was trying to believe what I had heard. My tiny glimpse of an insight? Enough?

I started to comprehend some of Thầy's song, "I have arrived. I am home." What I needed was not to go anywhere else. "I am at home with myself." Gradually, it was becoming possible to return home to myself, at least sometimes.

During our years together, Svein and I read the Five Awarenesses each month. Time and again, hearing those simple words and remembering the ceremony in which I had wholeheartedly committed to them reconnected me with my wiser self and helped me to let go of divisive impulses. I learned to notice the thought, *But I'm right and Svein is wrong!* arise in me and to simply watch it, knowing it was only one way of looking at the situation. This I was able to do. Having no ambition at work, however, was harder. The wisdom felt right, but I was a young academic on temporary contracts and had a strong habit energy of pushing myself too hard. Could I trust there would be a future job? Only take one small, hesitant step after the other?

Eleven years after our wedding, I returned to Plum Village and had another private meeting with Thầy. Svein had passed away a few months earlier, and I was grieving deeply. There were only a few ordinary things I felt capable of doing, yet no one needed to remind me of the miracle of walking on the Earth. Each step simply was. Years earlier I had heard Thầy speaking of this miracle, and now those teachings were in me, they *were* me.

The community in Plum Village's New Hamlet was infinitely gentle in easing my path. There was always a hammock available when I looked for one. Once, a Vietnamese laywoman I had never met made a child leave a hammock as I approached. There were so many signs that I was cared for in the community. Yet something prevented me from fully taking it in. Meeting with Thầy, I asked for advice about other things than what was truly in my heart, being too shy to probe the depths of my insecurity.

Embracing the pain in my being, I found words the next day. I wrote a letter to Thầy about our initial meeting years earlier when I had learned how to drink a cup of tea, how to have no ambition at work, and how deeply the community loved Svein. As gentle tears of letting go streamed down my face, I let the pen share with Thầy what I had been ashamed to voice even to myself: In Plum Village, I had always considered myself "Svein's wife." Now the question in my heart was: In what way could I be there for the community? And—the pen nearly refused to write—in what way was the community there for me?

Thầy's response was gentle, immense, and unspoken. A thundering silence. I never received an explicit reply, but over time he offered something deeper: his subtle attention. He saw me. Caught my eye in the crowd for a moment. Time and time again. For two summers, when life seemed to have lost its color, I drank the clear water of this quiet support.

During this period I received the Lamp Transmission; Thầy ordained me as a dharma teacher, as Svein had been. As part of the ceremony, we exchanged poems. This was a significant event, visible to many. Those moments of being seen touched me deeply. At first I found it hard to receive, but I gradually recognized a new depth of coming home to myself, of daring to fully receive.

Then one summer, soon after arriving in Plum Village, I was standing in a crowd inside a side door to the big meditation hall in Lower Hamlet, hands together to greet Thầy's arrival. Again that quick glance—one moment of full attention.

Then, no more.

I thought to myself, *Now it happens.* I've heard of this: the pain when he no longer sees you. Okay, here we go. But it didn't hurt—I could actually take it.

Days later, I understood. A single glance was enough for Thầy to see that I no longer depended on his support. He knew before I did! He saw me—deeply. I pondered the magnitude of this. What Thầy had been giving attention to was less an individual me than a suffering being with the capacity to heal. I was one of many, and Thầy's healing of me was part of his contribution to healing the world. The deep suffering was the point, and although my sense of myself as an individual still existed, the suffering I experienced had transformed. It was not about me, but about discovering there is also a non-me. All beings are interconnected, and I am no more and no less than a manifestation of all the non-me elements of the universe. This is what Thầy calls interbeing.

This insight completed a cycle of letting go that had started with Svein's guidance, had deepened my self-acceptance, and transformed the suffering of generations. To this day, memories of Thầy's silent compassion remind me of the transformative power of coming home to my true non-self.

Eevi Beck lives in Norway and practices with the Sangha of Floating Clouds in Oslo, as well as with a Science Sangha founded after the 2021 Plum Village Science retreat. She received the dharma name True Compassionate Practice when she was ordained into the Order of Interbeing and sees it as an invitation to develop deep compassion for others. Eevi was given the Dharma Lamp in 2008, which signifies that she is a dharma teacher in the Plum Village tradition. She was married to a dharma teacher for eleven years before becoming a widow in 2007 and practicing for years after that as a single mother. Eevi works as an academic at a university.

PART 4

Reconciliation:
Coming Back to Each Other

An Ex-Nun, Addiction,
and Forgiveness

by Joann Malone

IT WAS 1968, THE NIGHTLY body count in Vietnam growing, our anger and frustration with the war peaking. I was a Catholic nun, an organizer against the draft and the war since my first student had been killed there. I joined other activists and draft resisters one evening at a local college in St. Louis to hear a Vietnamese monk, recently exiled from his country, tell us how the war affected him. Thích Nhất Hạnh's description of the suffering of his people from US bombs shook me. I was deeply impressed by the way he responded to a heckler in the audience who shouted, "The war is in Vietnam, so why don't you go back there!" Thầy took a breath to drain anger from his body then looked at the man with amazing calm and said, "The root of the suffering in Vietnam is here, so I have come here to bring peace to you and thus to my people in Vietnam."

Thầy inspired me to take stronger action to end war. In 1969, outraged at our government and corporations profiting from war and sick at heart from seeing photos of napalmed children on television, I joined an action in

Washington, DC against the Dow Chemical Company. After careful planning to avoid harming anyone, five priests, an ex-nun, a young draft resister, and I broke into Dow's lobbying offices. Knowing that a police bullet might end our lives in this action, we linked arms, ready to do whatever it took to bring about peace in Vietnam. We trashed the office and then tossed files out the window to reporters waiting in the streets below. The documents were reprinted in major newspapers, exposing the profits Dow made from napalm, nerve gas, and defoliants that were killing people in Vietnam.

Drinking was part of the culture in the peace movement. It reduced the stress of our illegal activities and gave us false courage in the midst of our fears about prison. In long planning meetings for anti-war actions, I picked up the alcohol that had ruined my family and that I had avoided for many years by joining the convent. I had hoped to prevent myself from becoming like my alcoholic father, but with these comrades who drank and also had the nerve to act, I felt immune.

By this point I had left the convent and was raising a child as a single mother. As my anti-war and anti-racism work increased, and the support of my religious community disappeared, my drinking increased too. I picked up the habits of righteous anger, hatred of authority, and blaming the system for all my ills. By the time I came to a twelve-step recovery program in 1985, I had become a chronic, around-the-clock alcoholic. I was killing myself slowly—miserable, isolated, hating myself, and wanting to die.

Few people knew how much I suffered or how difficult it was to look in the mirror and no longer see the courage and self-sacrifice of my activist self. The man I lived with tried to kill me and threatened to kill my son. Fear and utter desolation finally drove me to seek help. Even if I no longer valued my life, I needed to find help to save my son. Unable to stop drinking on my own, I went to my first meeting for alcoholics. I heard an invitation to surrender and accepted help. After a few meetings, I experienced the miracle of twenty-four hours without a drink. The twelve-step programs not only helped me stop drinking but eventually led me to daily meditation. After working the steps and practicing meditation on my own for six years, I had a solid spiritual path. But I still longed for a community that practiced meditation together. I knew I needed to take care of my anger, shame, and blaming of my father for my alcoholism.

In 1991, my son told me about a retreat in Virginia he planned to attend. I signed up too, partly to spend the weekend with him. Preparing for the retreat, I read Thầy's *The Miracle of Mindfulness* and realized from the introduction that the retreat leader was the same monk I had met in 1968! In just one meeting he had changed my life dramatically and inspired me to expose Dow's complicity in the Vietnam war. What would happen to my life if he was my teacher?

At that retreat, and at many others since, I have learned how to come back to my breath, to calm my body and emotions, to relax, and to live in the present moment. Thầy said, "In this moment is everything—all of human history, all our ancestors, all future generations. In taking care of our own anger, fear, and despair, we transform the suffering of our ancestors, our children, and their children. We bring peace, joy, and love to the whole world!"

That world of peace was visible, tangible to me in the hall filled with hundreds of multi-national meditators. I was no longer trying to meditate alone; the energy of sitting with the large community of experienced monks, nuns, and others was so powerful! I have continued from that weekend retreat to practice regularly with a Sangha, daily with my husband, and on frequent retreats, especially the retreats that I lead for alcoholic women, where my two spiritual paths meet.

I found a harmony between my twelve-step spiritual program and Thầy's teachings. His words about impermanence fit with practices like "one day at a time" and "letting go" that I learned in recovery meetings. Mindfulness, stopping to breathe before acting, and living in the present moment in particular helped me with the twelfth step goal to "practice principles of love and tolerance in all our affairs." My thinking and behavior kept changing as I learned how much I am powerless over, especially other people's behavior.

I came slowly to see that anger and outrage at the behavior of others, at governments, even at war itself, was not enough to bring peace. I had to act from peace within myself, to change my own behavior in order to be useful in changing society and the world. I had to transform my relationships with everyone in my life. This included my father.

Carried in the arms of the worldwide Sangha, I gradually let go of blaming my father for my alcoholic suffering. After years of working the twelve steps, meditating daily, and practicing the Mindfulness Trainings, I had a particularly powerful retreat with Thầy in Italy. At large retreats

I usually formed a recovery group to provide a source of support for alcoholics, but due to miscommunication, I was unable to do so at this one. I realized that the alcoholic I needed to meet with that week was my father, who had died drunk in 1986. At the time, I had been sober for nine months. Throughout the retreat I ate, rested, and meditated with my father, smiling at this man who had so influenced me.

I imagined him next to me as I listened to my teacher explain that our parents are still in us, in our very DNA. "Look at your left hand and see your father present there in your skin, your blood, the life line on your palm." I felt the last of my hatred and anger at my father drain away as we walked silently together to the sea with Thầy and hundreds of other retreatants. As an active alcoholic, I had become my father; I knew his suffering as my own, and now his suffering was being transformed in me through my sobriety.

Gradually, feelings of love and compassion for my father arose in my heart, rather than the anger and blame I had carried for so many years whenever I thought of him. I also felt compassion for myself, an alcoholic like my father. In fact, if my recovery could change the direction of our family history, then I had the privilege of being a small part of that change. A negative view of my suffering became positive. This process of my transformation took many years, yet the fact that it happened in just one lifetime was amazing. Perhaps this same sense of acceptance could transform my efforts for peace in the world, helping me to see myself as one small cell in a great body of peacemakers whose work spanned centuries.

The obstacle had become the path. My alcoholism is not an obstacle to overcome in order to live my life; it is my life! It uniquely qualifies me to help others who suffer from my disease. I no longer feel I have to achieve a certain objective in order to make peace in my heart or in the world. I can have peace right here, right now, in every step of the process. The daily choices of sobriety, kindness, and deep listening, demonstrated by Thầy's interaction with the heckler so many years ago, transform my life and my choices as a daughter, an alcoholic, and an activist.

Joann Malone lives in the United States. She practices mainly with the Washington Mindfulness Community and was ordained into the Order of Interbeing in 2011. Joann loves her dharma name, Powerful Love of the Heart, since love has been a theme, a gift, and a central inspiration in her life. She says that all the love she has received opens her heart to continuously love others more. Joann's book, *AWAKE to Racism*, was published in 2021, and she explores the impact of her Irish Catholic alcoholic roots in an earlier book, *Dakota Winds*. After several years as a Catholic nun and twenty-seven years teaching high school, Joann has found more time for writing, conducting women's retreats for alcoholics, teaching meditation and Qi Gong, traveling, and local trouble making.

We Come from the
Same Quiet Place

by Nel Houtman

WHEN I FIRST VISITED PLUM VILLAGE, I was not yet aware that I had come to heal my wounds. I had followed my mother's footsteps to Thích Nhất Hạnh's community in France, unconsciously seeking help to repair my strained and broken-off relationship with my father. After many strict sesshins with Japanese Zen masters in the past, I knew I needed a gentler guide and a more gentle and loving inner approach to dealing with myself. My mother's recollections of the many mindfulness exercises in daily life at Plum Village incited my curiosity and presented the possibility of finding the spiritual guide I hoped for.

On this visit, I struggled with old wounds of not being seen by my father when I was growing up. He had been absorbed in his meditative praxis and his work, and I never knew whether or how he perceived me. His failure to acknowledge me made me feel totally disoriented and insecure.

There I was, sitting in the bamboo grove of the Lower Hamlet with a small group of Western seekers and a larger group of Vietnamese people, many of whom were grievously wounded refugees from Vietnam. At that time, Plum Village consisted of two hamlets, old French farmhouses that were transformed into two practice centers. A gentle breeze and warm sun rays caressed us as we gathered for a question and answer session with Thầy. When he spoke about handling difficult emotions, I suddenly heard myself say, "Thầy, I want to get rid of my hate for my father."

Thầy gave me a look that expressed both surprise and tenderness and spoke in clear, urgent words: "Don't throw away your hate; it is precious!"

A bomb went off inside me. Hate was supposed to be precious? My brain rattled. Part of me failed to understand, but another part grasped Thầy's profound meaning. The energy trapped in the hatred broke up and changed. That night, I wept for a long time and felt charged with intense emotions: love, coming home, a long phase of loneliness, an inner sense of fatherlessness, and grief.

Although this insight gave me more peace inside myself, I could not relate to my father.

On another visit to Plum Village many years later, I asked Thầy how I might really and fully recover from the pain of being invisible to my father. Thầy suggested that I travel to Indonesia, my father's birthplace, to become familiar with the country, practice walking meditation, and become familiar with the root energy of my father and his ancestors. *What kind of answer to my pain is that?* I thought. I even wondered whether Thầy had understood me properly. It seemed absurd and overly simple to just go without prior discussion, clearing the air, or receiving an apology from my father. However, something in the depths of my being understood. The seed of curiosity had been planted.

A few years later, when I had left my job and could afford to take off for three months, I traveled to Indonesia. During the first week after my arrival, I was utterly overwhelmed by the scents, the sounds, and the deeply religious atmosphere and was barely able to move. The sweet, heavy flower scent, the incense everywhere, the sounds of the Gamelan at night, the altars and religious rituals—all of it moved me deeply. Something in me cried for days. I did not understand what was happening to me.

All the gentle, quiet people I encountered, with their considerate manners and the habit to suddenly appear and disappear, reminded me so much of my father—the stillness that surrounded him, and his gaze, which always seemed to focus on something other than me and my brother.

One night, when I had grown calmer, I listened as the monsoon rain pattered on banana leaves. Except for the rain and a few frogs croaking far away, it was completely quiet. As I stood and listened, I suddenly felt my father's body within my own. His standing quietly in our house in the Netherlands became one with my standing quietly here in Java. The confines of time fell away, and I sensed the oneness of standing and listening with his younger self.

This reminded me of Thầy's teaching about interbeing, the idea that we all are interconnected and that relationships exist both across generations and across the illusion of birth and death. If we look and perceive deeply into our body, we can feel and meet our parents and ancestors in us. In this moment, alone in Java, time imploded into a single perception: the same for him and me. We listened to the stillness, we were the stillness.

I suddenly understood my father's quiet, absent ways. As a child, hungry for recognition and desperate to be seen, I had interpreted these ways as disinterest in me. I now experienced this stillness as paradise—the interwoven presence of all beings, things, and events. It was as though I was becoming part of the "ancient story," as my father used to say. He grew up in the stillness of nature and in tales from the *Bhagavad Gita*, told to him by his Javanese nanny. Behind all of this was his sense of being part of a continuum: no birth, no death. The ancient story, as my father called it, was the unstoppable life running through birth and death, ever changing and only grasped in moments of inner silence, when the interpreting mind finds home in the paradise of now.

With this gift of experience and understanding, I returned to the Netherlands and visited my father after seven painful years of separation. We drank tea together in a quiet restaurant in Amsterdam, and I told him of my experiences in Bali and Java. As I spoke, I felt his warmth, sympathy, and alert presence. Eventually, he said how sorry he was that he had not been a real father to me and that he had taken so little interest in my everyday childhood.

My father shared with me his own pain of being sent away by his parents as a young boy to attend a boarding school and later being separated from his mystical root country. I realized that my father's experiences of being banished from Java since World War II and enduring a Japanese concentration camp had caused him suffering but also brought many insights about life and death. I understood that all these experiences led him into his meditative practice. It dawned on me that the oneness behind all suffering and joy had been conveyed to me in silence.

I had not anticipated such an opening on his part, although I would have been overjoyed to hear it in earlier years. My insight into my father's behavior couldn't have happened before, because I had not yet understood that he and I come from the same quiet place. In my younger years, I could not make room for his silent communication. Now, although I no longer needed an explanation, his words helped to heal not only my wounds but also his own.

Nel Houtman lives in Switzerland. She learned how to meditate at the age of thirteen from her father, who was a Zen master, and her mother introduced her to the teachings of Thích Nhất Hạnh. In 1994, Nel was ordained into the Order of Interbeing and given the dharma name True Marvelous Shining, which is like her north star, pointing her back towards herself whenever she has lost her innate knowing and being. She infuses the mindfulness practice into her work as a body therapist, offering her clients an atmosphere of coming home to their true inner island. She has published articles in *Intersein*, the German Mindfulness Bell magazine. Much gratitude from Nel and the editors to **Dorothee Racette**, who translated this story, capturing the poetic way Nel intended it to sound.

My Five-Year-Old Father

by Dale William (Bill) Woodall

AS I SAT BY MY FATHER'S hospital bed about ten hours
before his death, the palliative care doctor had only one
question for me: "Is there any forgiveness to be shared
between you?" Intense joy came up immediately in my
heart and mind, because I knew the answer at once: "I
have only gratitude for my father and the efforts he made
to raise me." I left the room then so they could talk. My
gratitude continued to grow as I thought about Thích Nhất
Hạnh's teachings, which had brought me to this point. Ten
years prior, my thoughts and feelings would have been
quite different.

My emotional transformation started on a retreat in the
spring of 1996, the first such gathering for the Beginners
Mind Sangha in Boise, Idaho. This was my first retreat
of any kind, and by the second day, I wanted to be anywhere else. At the time, I was living alone in a log cabin
in the mountains; being in community was alien to me.
But I found in the shared silence a deep resonance, so I
stayed and practiced as deeply as I could. Then we did the
Three Earth Touchings, a ceremony that supports us in

recognizing the interconnection of all beings across space and time. During the first touching of the earth, we listened to a text that helped us connect with and be compassionate towards our spiritual and blood ancestors. Here are the lines in their current form, very similar to what I heard for the first time that day:

I know that parents always love and support their children and grandchildren, although they are not always able to express it skillfully because of difficulties they themselves encountered.

I cried when I heard these words, though I didn't have any insight into my feelings. The door that would lead to my transformation and healing opened slightly.

In spite of my difficulties being in community, I knew I had discovered something special in this Sangha, in the people who were there, and in Thích Nhất Hạnh's practice. Until then, my acquaintance with Buddhism had mostly been through a book by the Dalai Lama. While I found support in those writings, Thầy's teachings provided useful tools that helped me transform long-standing suffering. The earth-touching ceremony was one such tool that enabled me to open my perspective to the past and to understand that my "self" was more extensive and less separate than I realized. I remained in the community, and at the fall retreat that year I received the Five Mindfulness Trainings, guidelines to live life with more joy and less suffering. I continued studying on my own and with the Sangha.

In 2000, during a dharma talk at our spring retreat, we practiced seeing ourselves as five-year-old children. We were encouraged to hold that child with compassion, to look deeply into who he or she was, and thereby to gain insight into the experience of being that age in the time and place where we grew up. This practice was especially important for me, because I was in the midst of caring for my aging parents. I found a photograph of my father and me when I was five and focused on it during this practice.

As a five-year-old boy, I lived on a small ranch in southern Idaho. We raised hay, pasture, and grain to feed cattle, horses, chickens, and people. It was, as I came to understand later, a sustainable farm, one that my father operated instinctively and consciously based on a basic Buddhist principle: interbeing. From the tilling of the land and planting of seeds through to the harvest and the feeding and transport of cattle to market, everything was connected and needed to happen in the correct way. My father was mindful of every action and understood clearly that he had to be diligent every day to be financially successful.

As a little boy I didn't understand this. Even as I grew up and began to help on the farm, the implications of small mistakes weren't clear to me. Nor was it clear why I would be punished, sometimes harshly, for such mistakes. Herein was the source of misunderstanding and suffering. Simply put, my father tried to make me be perfect. I couldn't meet this standard, and it was hard on me.

The door that had been opened by the Touchings of the Earth widened as a result of my looking deeply into my young self. I felt some relief knowing that I was moving toward the heart of the matter: Why had my father treated me in this way? He was loving and supportive in other ways. He showed me that work was a valuable, enjoyable activity for its own sake, not merely for the money it brought in to pay the bills. On many occasions, he and I worked hard together at fixing a fence or stacking hay or cutting firewood, and we enjoyed the accomplishments and the solid tiredness such effort brings. "That's a good job well done," he would say as we headed in for supper.

The next part of the practice was to see my father as a small boy. After many months, the dharma door swung fully open for me. My father, who was born in 1918, lost his own father when he was five. As the last of seven brothers, he experienced a life far more difficult than mine. He was eleven when the Great Depression hit. He left school at fourteen to start working full time. He worked on ranches, road construction, and eventually on railroad construction during the early part of World War II. The lesson he learned during his adolescence and young manhood was very simple: if you made a mistake, it could all fall apart. You could lose everything you had.

When he left construction and returned to ranching in Idaho, he did lose everything, more than once. Life taught him hard lessons about interbeing: A patch of hay field that wasn't producing well meant less hay to be baled up. Hay bales that weren't cured properly meant the cows would have less milk for their calves. Those calves wouldn't gain as much weight as they might have, so when it came time to sell them in the fall, they brought in less money. All of this meant fewer resources for the family as we struggled through another winter.

My father's story had new meaning when I viewed it through the lens of this practice. He gave me what he thought I needed to be successful in life. He tried his best to prepare me for any difficulties I might encounter based upon what he had learned. Every time he encouraged me towards perfection, it was a deep manifestation of his love for me. This was one way he could express it, when so many other ways weren't possible for him.

With this realization, I was through the door of understanding, and the suffering I had felt in my relationship with him was fully transformed. With mindfulness based in deep gratitude and compassion, I was able to help him grow old, get sick, and die over the course of five years. About two weeks before he died, I was with him in the emergency room. He had pneumonia and his body was failing rapidly. The doctor asked if we should try to pull him back or let him go. My father couldn't answer; he just looked at me. I chose to have them save him, which proved to be important—he had two more evenings with my mother before he died.

When I left his room two weeks later to give the palliative care doctor time alone with him, my gratitude was combined with joy. I felt gratitude for my father and for Thầy's teachings, which had been so helpful to me and, through me, to my father. I felt joy that, in that moment, my feet were firmly on the path of understanding and compassion.

On January 1, 2022, **Dale William (Bill) Woodall** died after a brief bout with pancreatic cancer. We are deeply grateful for his message of kindness and peace, which lives on in his many family members and friends as well as in this book. Bill lived in the United States and practiced with the Beginner's Mind Sangha in Boise, Idaho. He was ordained into the Order of

Interbeing in 1997 and given the name True Healing of the Source. Bill was a dharma teacher, carpenter, writer, musician, loving husband, sibling, step-dad, and proud grandfather. At the time of his passing, Bill was working on his autobiography with the help of his dear friends Rick and Rosemary Ardinger.

Us vs. Them:
Letting Go of Sides

by John Bell

IRONICALLY, AS A LIFELONG WAR PROTESTER, I have
a war to thank for bringing Thích Nhất Hạnh into my life.
Our connection began in 1966, long before we actually
met. I was twenty-two years old and just graduating college. I faced the military draft, which could send me to
Vietnam as a US soldier. Thầy, at forty, had already been a
monk for twenty-four years and was building the School of
Youth for Social Service—thousands of courageous young
people dedicated to relieving suffering on both sides of the
conflict.

Thầy was suspect in his country because officials
thought he was sympathizing with the enemy. They were
right, although he called it compassion. He did not believe
in killing. Likewise, I was suspect in my country because
I did not believe in killing. I stood with millions of young
people to try to stop our part of the war. The United States
was committing unspeakable violence against the Vietnamese people. I marched, participated in nonviolent civil
disobedience protests, was tear-gassed and arrested.

Day after day, my young friends and I watched heart-breaking images on TV—endless streams of bombs dropping from B52s, fiery explosions on radiant green below, napalmed bodies and scorched villages, and the horrifying photo of the Buddhist monk who set himself on fire in protest. I knew that the war was deeply wrong.

Instead of going to war, I began teaching US History in high school in the fall of 1966. It turned out that teaching high school was considered a "national defense industry," which made me exempt from the draft. I still opposed the war, so what did I do? I began the school year with a unit of study on it.

During this period, the army drafted my younger brother, Mike, and sent him to Vietnam. He had not done well in high school and had dropped out of community college afterward. Mike was not critical of the war. Like many US families at the time, ours was split by having one soldier son and one protesting son. While I was teaching young people about the Vietnam War as best I could, Mike was driving supply truck convoys to the front lines near Pleiku as best he could. At the same time, Thích Nhất Hạnh and his friends were helping people rebuild villages and treating napalm burns as best they could.

One morning, in the middle of class, the loudspeaker boomed: "Mr. Bell, please report to the principal's office immediately!" When I arrived, a man in an Air Force uniform was standing there, fuming. He was the father of Linda, one of my students, and the commander of the local Air Force base. He had recently returned from a tour as a pilot in Vietnam. In my history class the day before, Linda, a sensitive girl, had listened to a guest speaker talk about the anti-personnel bombs used in Vietnam that drove bits of shrapnel deep into anything and anyone nearby. The speaker gave graphic descriptions of how the shrapnel tore through people. Horrified, she went home and asked her father if that was true. His response was indignation at me. "How dare you fill the minds of the students with propaganda!" he fumed. "I'm going to have you reprimanded!"

At the end of that school year I was fired for "being too young and too radical," even though I had tried my best to incorporate multiple viewpoints of the war into my history class. That same year, my brother came back from Vietnam, and Thầy began his thirty-nine-year exile from Vietnam. My brother, basically a tender-hearted young man, had been led by the conditions of war to commit heart-wrenching violence against Vietnamese people. He returned traumatized and felt unwelcome in his own country. I listened to his stories with as much compassion as I could, feeling even more deeply the fundamental wrongness of the war.

Meanwhile, although Thầy was now exiled from Vietnam, he had cultivated a deep mindfulness practice and could be "home" anywhere. He lived for decades in France, participated in the Paris peace talks that ended the war, assisted boat people escaping the war, continued to support practitioners in Vietnam from a distance, and always worked for inner and outer peace.

Over the next decade, I continued to protest the Vietnam War until it ended. I lived in Harlem and taught Black and Latino young people in community schools, helped organize against the US intervention in Central America, and worked for the abolition of nuclear weapons. These years were both exhilarating and exhausting. Exhilarating because I was working alongside people of all races and backgrounds who were trying to create a more humane, just, and peaceful world. Exhausting because we had very few ways of healing our grief, discouragement, fear, and anger about these injustices. I worked with peace activists who were not peaceful and with human rights workers who couldn't extend rights to all humans. Many social justice activists were caught in an "us vs. them" kind of dualism. I knew something was missing.

I finally found that missing piece when I met Thầy in 1982 in New York City. I had helped organize a conference of spiritual teachers called Reverence for Life, which was held the day before a peace march to abolish nuclear weapons. Thầy, one of the speakers, said three things that touched me. First was the suggestion to breathe three times before answering the phone in order to be more present for whoever is calling. Second, he posed a question: "What if the world agreed to have one day on which no one would go hungry?" This seemingly simple proposal masked the great changes that would have to take place for this to happen. This was revolution posing as a good idea. Brilliant!

Third, Thầy told a story about the refugees who escaped Vietnam by boat. Thirty or forty people would crowd onto a small fishing boat to cross the sea to Thailand. If a storm came up during the journey, the people would run in panic to one side of the boat or the other. That action in a rough sea would often capsize the boat and they would perish. But, Thầy explained, if there was one among them who could sit calmly in the boat while the storm raged, their example could calm others, and the group could ride out the storm to safety. Thầy asked the audience, "Who among us can sit calmly through the storms of our day?" This spoke volumes to me about the need not to just work for peace, but to be peace.

That day, I began my slow and inexorable process of becoming first a student of Thích Nhất Hạnh and then a teacher in his tradition—a continuation of him, for which I am deeply grateful. I was drawn to Thầy initially because he had emerged from the cauldron of the Vietnam War. Then, as I began to attend retreats, I came to see that he was an authentic human being without a huge ego; he was peaceful in himself. I could see that he obviously wanted to apply the teachings to real suffering in the present: he offered retreats and teachings for Vietnam veterans, for people in law enforcement, for people in prisons, for Palestinian and Jewish Israelis, and later for the World Bank, the US Congress, and various businesses. He was the teacher and the way of being that I had been looking for and had long tried to emulate, even before I met him.

Over the years, I experienced the blessing of watching Thầy work with Vietnam War veterans at retreats. Listening to my brother's war stories, I knew the deep hurt among vets who witnessed and did terrible things under life-and-death pressure. My brother has never healed from it. At retreats, Thầy would invite veteran after veteran to come up on the stage and sit face-to-face with a Vietnamese monastic. The vets would sob with remorse, guilt, and heartbreaking suffering as they asked for forgiveness. As the dharma hall swam in tears, hearts healed before our eyes. I wish my brother could have been among those vets.

Thầy's capacity to hold the suffering of those who caused him and his people so much pain showed me that I too can continue to act against war; I can continue to help all who are affected by it, regardless of the side they are on.

John Bell lives in the United States and practices with the Mountain Bell Sangha in the Boston area, the online sanghas Listening Circle for Healing Our White Racism, Earth Holder Regional Community Builders, and Dharma Teachers Conversations. He was ordained into the Order of Interbeing in 2001, receiving the name True Wonderful Wisdom. Having dedicated his life to justice, healing, and spiritual depth, John is writing a book titled *Unbroken Wholeness: Integrating Social Justice, Emotional Healing, and Spiritual Practice.* He has been happily partnered for fifty-two years and is a father, grandfather, and good ancestor.

PART 5

Facing Fear

What If, What If, What If?

by Jindra Čekanlová

GROWING UP, FEAR WAS MY constant companion, but
far from a friend. I dwelled on perceived threats, large and
small, because they all loomed large to me. What would
happen if my mother hurt herself while falling-down
drunk? What if my father's plane crashed while he was
traveling in the jungles of Borneo, Indonesia? What if he
went bankrupt again and I had to leave private school?
What if I finally failed my math class? What if the boy I
liked didn't invite me to the school dance? What if he did?

I tried to control my fears. When I was little, I covered
all my stuffed animals and dolls with small pieces of cloth
to keep them safe. Raised Roman Catholic, I prayed. But
seeing what God wrought on Earth, I eventually left the
Church. I began to explore different faiths, looking for a
way to spiritually survive and to deal with my emotions.

As a teen, I tried to calm myself through running and
turned my focus to my body. I taught myself not to hyper-
ventilate about the things that scared me by planning and
forecasting as I ran. I projected what everyone would say

and do, and I practiced clear ways I would respond in each scenario. What if, what if, what if? Then, then, then. I made and remade contingency plans for everything, from physical harm to penury, from failing out of school to becoming pregnant or being infertile. My careful planning helped me cope with fear, though it could not always prevent awfulness from happening.

During graduate work in the United Kingdom, France, and Mali, I tried to manage my fears by trying to manage other people's crises. I examined how people's livelihoods in rural Africa saved them from famine and projected how we could help. But trying to control everything was exhausting. A fellow student suggested I calm my anxiety by joining his Zen meditation group. I found focusing on my breath helped, yet with my next job, I was right back at square one. Jon Kabat-Zinn's *Wherever You Go, There You Are* was right: soon I was clocking eighty hours a week, afraid to do less and too tired to meditate.

In 1994, I moved to Washington, DC, and found Thích Nhất Hạnh's practice. I watched my fearful thoughts arise but did not try to manage them or run from them. I just watched. Listening to Thầy and the monastics and reading his books, including one he must have written for me—*Fear*—I learned to breathe and to really know I was breathing. I watched the chaos of my thoughts and began to forgive their raging. I watched my inability to sit by returning to my breath impatiently for the thousandth time, experiencing only five of ten breaths, and getting lost again. I judged myself harshly. I was afraid I wasn't good enough to do this. But with the wisdom of the Sangha and through dharma sharing, I learned to watch fear arise in the present moment and to see myself with more compassion. I sat, I walked, I judged, I watched boredom, frustration, and fear arise. I forgave myself one moment, dozed in the next, then itched, then planned, then caught myself planning. Increasingly, I felt peace in tiny but repeated respites.

I practiced walking meditation: placing each foot mindfully, in tune with my slow breath as Thầy taught us. I did it in a war-torn country, in a wide-open desert, and in bustling cities, and in a variety of meditation spaces. I came to see that it was never the place, but the practitioner that mattered. The same fears traveled with me, as did practices to watch them and even befriend them. My mind could be calm in a Kosovo war zone but agitated at Blue Cliff Monastery's lotus pond. I could be compassionately peaceful at a border crossing but angrily impatient with fellow meditation retreatants.

Eventually, I practiced my way out of my life-long controlling anxiety using The Fourteen Mindfulness Trainings as a guide. Thầy wrote these in 1966 in Saigon as a roadmap for the layperson to live life joyfully.

The Sixth Mindfulness Training teaches us to "Practice Right Diligence to nourish our capacity of understanding, love, joy, and inclusiveness, gradually transforming our anger, violence, and fear and helping others do the same." As I reflected on this training, I came to see that my parents could not avoid transferring their own fears to me. As World War II refugees and immigrants, they came from conditions of trauma; they were filled with fear and knew no other way than inflicting harm on themselves and each other. They never had the fortune to encounter the wisdom and freedom from fear that meditation provided me.

This training gave me signposts for how to put my fears into perspective. It showed me how to get beyond my fear by bringing my awareness to the conditions that feed anger, violence, and fear, as well as to those that feed understanding, love, joy, and inclusiveness. When my negative emotions arise, I notice them and then carefully water the positive seeds in my consciousness rather than the fearful, negative ones. By doing so, I can retrain my mind and choose presence over planning. My practice saved me by helping me to realize that all I have is now, not a feared future.

In 2011, my adult daughter Jirinka and I were having coffee at the base of Mont Tremblant, in Canada, while my younger sons snowboarded at a ski school on the slopes above us. Suddenly, a call. My nine-year-old son Erik was being brought down by the ski patrol with a concussion and possibly a spinal injury. I sprinted to the ski station, yelling to Jirinka to find my other son Kaja and bring him to the hotel. Seeing my slender son strapped down, immobile, my heart pounded, and horrific scenarios appeared in quick succession in my mind.

We were transported to the hospital for tests. I smoothed his matted red hair off his brow, careful not to touch the neck brace. Repeatedly I replaced the terrible thoughts that snowballed in my mind with Thầy's mantra, "Breathing in, I know that I am breathing in. Breathing out, I know that I am breathing out." I continued to repeat these words silently. Erik complained he needed to use the toilet but he was not sure they would let him get up, so I suggested he "not think wet thoughts." We smiled wanly. I realized then that all I had was that very moment, that shared instant with him. If we had no other, no "normal" moment, I would not waste this one in fear. Nor the next, nor the next. I pressed his hand, saying, "No matter what, it will be okay, Eri."

I distracted him from his discomfort by telling him stories—of how herders believed there were spirits under the dry dunes in Mali and how they protected themselves with amulets. I told him how afraid I had been after my scoliosis operation, lying in a body cast like his, and how great it had felt when I finally got to stand up and walk. He would too. We both avoided the story, for that moment, of how this had happened to him.

During silences I drew on my twenty years of practice and grounded myself in my breath to hold the fear as it arose and faded, arose and faded. Fear could have flooded me and taken me to some imagined and horrible Erik future of wheelchairs, breathing tanks, and a shortened life if I let it. That fear would have taken me away from my son, who rested next to me in the here and now.

I returned to my breath hundreds of times in the six hours it took for them to diagnose a severe concussion but no paralysis. Finally, we were given a bottle he could pee in. Later, nurses returned to unstrap him. After more tests and hours, we were allowed to go home. Jirinka and Kaja hugged Erik gingerly. That night I went to bed more grateful for his health than ever, and grateful for the fact that I had been there fully for and with him.

Thích Nhất Hạnh says that when we encounter difficult emotions we can "return to our body, as our suffering child is calling us." By going back to my breath and feeling the fear arise, I can hold it. I can touch the fear and then let it go repeatedly, as I did in the hospital that day.

Jindra Čekanlova lives in the Czech Republic and practices with the Czech Republic Plum Village Sangha, the Oak Tree Sangha in Europe, and virtually with the Washington Mindfulness Community and the Stillwater Mindfulness Practice Center in Maryland. Ordained into the Order of Interbeing in 2011, she says her dharma name, True Collective Maintenance, reflects her sense that she is the plumber of the Sangha, making sure dharma flows. Jindra has written articles on Buddhism for the *Mindfulness Bell*, and she has spent time in many countries around the globe as a professional in international development.

Phew!
What a Wonderful Colon I Have!

by Katie Sheen

PHEW! *What a wonderful colon I have*, I think. On the monitor screen it looks healthy, and the consultant doing the colonoscopy seems happy and chatty.

"We'll just turn the camera around and look back at the last little part, to double check that area," she says, and suddenly there it is. A gaping wound, with strange, gently bleeding little nodules around it. There is a slight pause, a missed beat in the conversation.

"We'll take six biopsies from this area," she says, trying to be brave. A thin metal instrument slides into view on the screen and starts to take little bites from the nodules and from around the wound.

I close my eyes and find my attention automatically searching out the sensations of breathing within my body, looking for comfort, for that peaceful core of inner strength that has been gradually building over years of practice with my Plum Village Sangha, Thích Nhất Hạnh's community of practice.

> Breathing in, I know that I am breathing in.
> Breathing out, I know that I am breathing out.

On the in breath, I say "In."
On the out breath, I say "Out."

> *In, out*
> *In, out*
> *In, out*

In the midst of strong emotion, my breathing is safe and familiar. The slight pause between the out breath and the in breath is always a peaceful place that remains secure, even when I feel adrenaline rising and emotions beginning to surge.

I notice shock, a kind of nothing feeling, an emotional pause between life before and life after this moment.

> Breathing in, I am aware of my feeling of shock.
> Breathing out, I take care of my feeling of shock.
> *Aware, taking care*

I seem to be crying, but it's just a few tears, gently rolling down my cheeks. I am silent, breathing, whilst they finish taking the biopsies.

> Breathing in, I am aware of my tears.
> Breathing out, I take care of my tears.
> *Aware, taking care*

At least I qualify for free art therapy now! I've always fancied having a go at that, and it really helped my brother-in-law Paul when he was first diagnosed with brain cancer.

> Breathing in, I am aware of my random thought and
> seemingly inappropriate feeling of happiness.
> Breathing out, I smile and take care of my happiness.
> *Aware, taking care*

Paul died though, aged just thirty-five years old. My sister, her children, my children, our parents, our whole family was devastated. What if I die too and they have to go through all of that again? That would break my heart as well as theirs.

> Breathing in, I am aware of panic starting to arise.
> Breathing out, I take care of the panic.
> *Aware, taking care*

The panic starts to settle down and for now, I'm not quite sure how I feel.

> Breathing in, I know that I am breathing in.
> Breathing out, I know that I am breathing out.
> *In, out*

The consultant has finished the procedures. She has taken off her gloves and washed her hands. There is slightly hushed, practical chat between her and the other nurses in the room. She walks around to my head, as I am still lying on my side, a sheet now pulled down to cover my legs. She takes my hand and looks into my eyes.

"What else could it be?" I ask.

"We'll have to wait for the results of the biopsies," she says.

We look at each other. We both know it could be nothing else except cancer, but in her eyes, in the strength of her hand around mine, I can feel that she wants me to survive. That she is sorry for what we have just discovered together. That her support, concern, and care for me are absolutely unconditional. All those things I had tried so hard to achieve and all I had struggled to be are suddenly irrelevant; we haven't known each other long enough for her to know about them. In that moment, it is just one human being connecting with another and willing them to stay alive. To keep breathing.

Katie Sheen lives in the United Kingdom and practices with the Being Peace Sangha, which is working to manifest Thầy's vision of a practice center in the UK, and with Sangha in the Peak. Katie was diagnosed with anal cancer on November 4th, 2014, treated with radiotherapy and chemotherapy in 2015, and consequently cured. Inspired by how Thầy's teachings supported her, she now teaches mindfulness to both health practitioners and the general public, and she is a course leader for Plum Village UK. Her dharma name, Dharma Light of the Heart, reminds her that at the foundation of her teaching is her own practice, which is gradually bringing a stronger light and lightness into her own heart. Katie has two wonderful sons and enjoys pottering in the garden, listening to birdsong, and walking with treasured friends and family amongst the hills and lakes.

Raging with Reason

by Marilyn J. Rivers

WHILE BROWSING IN A THRIFT SHOP, I suddenly felt electrical currents running into my hand and up my arm. These sensations beckoned me to move my hand in the direction of a cassette tape on the table before me. The cover of the tape said "Peace-Making: How to Be It; How to Do It," by Thích Nhất Hạnh. I spent a few dollars to buy it.

It wasn't like I had lots of money. I was a newly-single mother of a too-smart kid, and scraping enough together each week to feed us was a challenge. Still, Thầy beckoned.

I listened to the tape right away—and was disappointed. I was looking for help dealing with anger, and here was a Buddhist monk talking about non-duality in a calm, soothing voice, repeating a single phrase over and over: "This is like this, because that is like that." It seemed like he was proposing that all anger had a cause and we just needed to discover that cause to stop it. He even admitted his own anger!

"Anger is me," he said. "I am anger."

"Well of course you are," I addressed his voice, gesticulating into the air. "You'd have to be crazy not to feel anger living in this world!"

My own rage was close to the surface in those days. Something in Thầy's matter-of-fact presentation set me off, triggered the sense of unfairness I had lived with most of my life. It was hard to listen to him, and yet something compelled me to keep playing that tape, day after day.

"Who are you going to sell this to?" I asked him, forgetting I was the one who had bought the tape and memorized nearly every word of it.

It may have been my imagination, but more than once I heard him laughing somewhere in my head—a low tinkle of jingling mirth emanating from the belly—no choice, I had to smile. As I smiled, my body felt as if it were being compassionately and warmly held with as much love as I had ever felt. Thầy's deep and giving nature had found a home in my inner realms. The sound of his laughter, an extension of his voice, resonated in my body as awareness of the compassion he felt for all of life.

In my job at the time, I led group counseling sessions with men, where we discussed the abuse and violence they had been charged with inflicting on women and children in their lives. As a survivor of childhood trauma, I still felt angry over my own experiences, yet I was working with people whose anger had taken them to very dark places. The irony was not lost on me. For some reason, I was comfortable with these men and they seemed to be okay with me, even when I challenged them. This was so unusual that the agency personnel running the groups had come to view me as someone to keep around. Although I had chanced upon this work while taking a college course between undergrad and graduate degrees, I began to see what I was doing with the men as more than random—it was a gift of healing for the healer.

Most of the group participants I worked with had been sent to the agency after being arrested for assault, and they tended to be filled with anger at being accused of intending to harm their loved ones. According to them, the courts were biased against men—they claimed women called the police frivolously when they were losing an argument or just wanted to get their way. In the 1990s, Canada's provincial police were primarily male and often agreed with the clients, which made my work helping the men take responsibility for their behavior even harder. The government had just initiated public policy in 1993 requiring police to lay charges if there was evidence indicating a woman had been physically interfered with. However, it would take many years for it to become common knowledge why this was necessary. Most men, regardless of class or race, had a sense of entitlement over their families that allowed for "small" acts of violence. The men saw it as necessary to maintain control. Naturally, losing that control created anger. Although I knew that, as a woman, my anger had not come from a sense of entitlement, it became clear to me that I had a few things in common with my clients.

This is where Thầy was so comforting. He taught that the greatest sources of anger come from feelings of being unfairly treated, especially when combined with fear of the injustices that permeate our world. He helped me see my clients as raging with reason—raging at being interrupted in what they believed was their job of heading a household.

Fear was a natural response to this disturbance. They feared for their family and their way of life. The therapy group was the one place where someone might listen, sometimes even a facilitator like me.

Thầy's tape offered me a pathway to the inner sanctum of men's psyches. He talked about abuse in the larger framework of oppression on the world stage, where he was intimately acquainted with relationships between nations. Vietnam, the country of his birth, had been torn apart, North from South, by the fears of the United States and the Soviet Union. These powerful nations had insisted on war rather than peace, using Thầy's homeland as their battleground. This reminded me of the family dynamics I dealt with in the men's groups, where the children got caught in the middle. It seemed that every man was quick to blame the woman involved, but no one wanted to be seen as blaming children. So just as the United States blamed the Soviet Union, so too did the Soviets blame the Americans. And both refused to initiate peace for fear of being seen as weak and losing the advantage of a foothold for conflict. From Thầy's teaching, I could clearly see that it was fear, not strength, that created the need for conflict in the first place. I began to understand a deeper reality.

A door opened for me to really listen to the men I was working with, and when I did, I heard fear. In many cases, the deepest fear was that of losing the relationships that meant the most to them, the ones they were destroying with abuse. Like powerful nations, these men did not know how to be powerful in any way other than a physical one. They kept doing more of what was hurting everyone, while expecting it to end the hurt. I learned to stop recoiling from the harm they had inflicted and to focus instead on the source of that harm. Thầy wanted the US and Soviet powers to get together and feed the hungry throughout Vietnam and to stop selling ammunition to the citizens of both the North and the South. He wanted them to give the people reasons to live rather than to die. I learned to deliver a similar message focused on the good of the whole and speaking to the inner child in men secretly aghast at their own behavior. Every man had been a child once and knew what it was like to be bullied. Many had vowed never to behave that way, especially if the bully in their early life had been a close family member.

Of course this was not a panacea for everyone. Not every man I worked with walked through the door Thầy's teachings held open; enough did, however, to keep me dedicated for many years. Like Thầy, I became a peacemaker. He taught me how to be it and how to do it, just as his cassette tape had promised my skeptical ears so many years before. As an effect of our combined efforts, thousands of people have accessed the benefits. For not only did my clients receive Thầy's learning, but so did every one of their family members who did the hard work of building trust again.

Marilyn J. Rivers first became involved with Buddhism in the early 1990s in Toronto, Canada with a Vipassana-focused Sangha in the Shambhala tradition. There, she took the Bodhisattva Vow and was given the name Enlightenment Divine Torch. For her, the word torch is an indication that she can be a leader at times, and it also refers to the many challenging questions she tends to ask her teachers. In 2017, Marilyn moved north to the countryside and began practicing on the shores of the Georgian Bay with the Heron Croft Sangha, composed primarily of students practicing in Thích Nhất Hạnh's tradition. Marilyn is a licensed psychotherapist working in private practice. She wrote magazine and newspaper articles in the 1980s and has more recently focused on poetry, with several poems published in a local anthology. Grateful to her son for his support of her practice, Marilyn notes that her commitment to meditation and to Thầy's teachings transformed her anger so that she did not pass it on to her son.

PART 6

Loss and Grief

The Last Time I Saw My Son, Alex

by Teresa L. Waller

I LAST SAW MY SON, Alex, on October 15, 2016, when he and his girlfriend, Sarah, came to my hometown in Madison, Indiana, to attend an art show reception that was very important to me. Alex, who had struggled with drug addiction and depression for many years, seemed to be entering a positive period. He was the picture of health, smiling and giving me a warm hug and saying "I love you" before he walked out of the gallery to return to Bloomington. Little did I know it would be the last time I would see this beautiful, intelligent, loving young man alive.

The next afternoon, Sarah texted me: "I don't want to worry you, but I haven't heard from Alex since around 6:30 last night." My gut told me that something was very wrong. She had messaged me from work and was unable to leave for another four hours. I began calling, texting, and messaging Alex's friends, with no luck. Eventually, I persuaded the weekend staff of the property management company to go by Alex's apartment to see if his car was there. They called back to tell me that yes, his car was in the parking lot. They had knocked on the door, but he didn't answer. It was then that I knew Alex was dead. After I called the police, it was an agonizing wait of several more hours until the coroner called to tell me that the police broke down the door and found Alex. There was no obvious cause, but he had likely died the evening before when he suddenly stopped texting Sarah.

In the immediate aftermath of Alex's death, there were many challenging events with which I had no first-hand experience. Among my first actions were phone calls to notify loved ones: Alex's father, my parents, Alex's friends, and my close friends. They had to be contacted immediately. Mercifully, there was no time to ruminate on what to say or how to say it.

My mindfulness practice was only a few months old, and I had not yet found a Sangha. Still, I was able to practice breathing to stay calm throughout the long ordeal of waiting to know what happened to Alex and in the immediate aftermath of the most dreaded event in a parent's life. I often reflect that, had Alex's death occurred prior to my learning of Thích Nhất Hạnh's teachings, my response to the loss would have been very different. From that day forward, I lived as if Thầy was holding my hand, helping me to remember to be present with my breath. My practice was no longer a mere intellectual and casual interest; it was a life-saving parachute as I fell into the abyss of despair.

The worst day was going to the funeral home with Alex's father. I used the practice of Pebble Meditation to calm my racing heart before going inside to view my dear son's body. In this meditation, I held four pebbles in my hand. I focused on one at a time to represent the freshness of a flower, the solidity of a mountain, the reality of a clear lake, and the spaciousness of open space. Doing this, my heart rate went from the mid 120s down to the 70s. It was enough to allow me to proceed with the most difficult duty of my life.

Going into the funeral home was surreal—we had not yet seen proof that our child was dead. That moment is forever emblazoned in my memory. Walking into the carpeted room holding Alex's father's hand, feeling as though my legs would not support me; catching sight of our perfect, beautiful boy lying serenely on the gurney, dressed in a hospital gown, hands folded on his tummy. His long flowing hair was freshly washed and dried, his body cold but perfect in every way. Soon my father and stepmother, my partner, my best friend, and Alex's girlfriend entered the room. There is no way to describe the agony of seeing my father cry at the loss of his only grandchild. If ever I was going to drop dead, that would have been the day.

One week after Alex's death, I attended my first Day of Mindfulness with the Louisville Community of Mindful Living. During dharma sharing, I put my sorrow into the middle of the circle. Afterward, a woman came up to me and shared that she had lost her son three years before. Her compassion and the Sangha's understanding were very comforting; I felt enveloped by love and truly at home.

Though Louisville is an hour's drive from my hometown, I began attending Sangha regularly, rarely missing Sunday practice. Certainly, the love and support of family and friends were a tremendous comfort, but Thầy's teachings and the presence of the Sangha enabled me to find inner strength. I don't know what I would have done without my Sangha brothers and sisters.

People say things like, "I could never survive the loss of my child" or ask me, "How did you get through it?" These are things that once ran through my own mind. The answer is difficult for me to articulate. Both specific moments of practice and insight as well as the gestalt of the teachings have been my parachute.

Understanding interbeing has helped me tremendously. I was inspired by the knowledge that my son didn't just disappear; as Thầy points out, science proves that nothing is lost. Like the flame at the tip of a match, though it is no longer visible when we blow it out, the elements of that flame are still there. And so is Alex.

The lesson of the second arrow helped me to recognize that the primary pain I felt from Alex's death need not be amplified. Adding a story of guilt and anger, which the Buddha refers to as a second arrow we fire upon ourselves, only deepens a wound I already have. I learned to call my suffering by its true name—grief—and to take care of it with love, understanding, and compassion. I learned that joy and grief are two sides of the same coin; it is okay to be happy while also grieving for my son.

I appreciated Thầy's honesty when he wrote about grieving the death of his mother for a whole year. Thầy also described a dream of being with his mother when she was young and healthy. When he awoke and walked in the moonlight, he felt his mother's presence and realized she was very much alive in him and around him. This story allowed me to see the same truth about Alex.

After a torturous wait of more than a month, we finally learned that Alex died of an opiate overdose. We were aware that he had been legally buying a powerful opiate from China, but, to our knowledge, he had stopped several months before his death. Because of Thầy's teachings, I have never entertained the question "Why me?" Rather, I say "Why not me?" and "What can I do to help?"

I speak openly of how the practice has helped me navigate the complex emotions of grief, anger, and loss and how it has allowed compassion to bloom. Inspired to share within my own community, I started the Flowing River Community of Mindful Living in my hometown. We practice compassion for ourselves and for others, understanding that one person's suffering and the suffering of others are not separate.

***

Teresa L. Waller lives in the United States with her partner Arti Ortega. She founded the Flowing River Community of Mindful Living in Madison, Indiana, in 2018 and also practices with the Louisville Community of Mindful Living in Kentucky and the Being Peace Sangha in Cincinnati, Ohio. Her dharma name is Healing Presence of the Heart, which she received a year after her son, Alex, died. She was on retreat at Magnolia Grove Monastery and participated in a grief and loss affinity group called the Be Brave family. The group grew close and had a touching ceremony of placing some of Alex's ashes outside the meditation hall, beside the spot where they met regularly. Teresa's dharma name perfectly captures the healing she experienced through the presence of community. With her passion for supporting mindfulness and the creative arts in her hometown, Teresa is a partner in Studio Be, which offers yoga, sound journeys, drumming, and mindfulness. She enjoys painting and drawing, and her artwork has been exhibited in galleries in Indiana and Kentucky.

Freedom from My Own Mind

by Joanne Friday

UNABLE TO REMEMBER ANYTHING or regulate my stress hormones, I was trapped in a constant state of anxiety and fear. I had been in a car accident that caused a life-changing brain injury.

About a year earlier, a friend had given me Thầy's book *The Miracle of Mindfulness* to help me cope with a very stressful job. Each night before I went to sleep, Thầy's words calmed me. Though I read the first half of the book over and over, I had been too busy, in my own mind, to use the wonderful practices Thầy offered in the last half. I didn't have time.

A few months after the car accident, I saw Thầy in a photo advertising a retreat near where I live in Rhode Island. Recognizing him from the cover of the book I had read so many times, I thought, *I should go there*. Because of the brain injury, I had become a totally concrete thinker with no ability to intellectualize. So, never having done anything like it before, I found myself at a week-long retreat.

It was the perfect thing to do. Thầy spoke of being fully in the present moment: the past is history and the future has not yet arrived, so this present moment is all we have. Since I had no memory of the past and was in fear of going forward in my life with no ability to think or function well, I loved the idea of focusing fully on the present.

Although my doctor told me to walk every day, ruptured discs from the car accident made every step painful. I focused on the pain and allowed my mind to go off into fear and speculation that my life was over. At the end of every walk, I felt much worse.

This was the opposite of walking meditation, which I discovered at the retreat with Thầy. Walking slowly outdoors, Thầy encouraged us to focus on the miracle of being a part of everything—interbeing. He reminded us that the trees exhaled what we inhaled, and we exhaled what the trees inhaled. When we focus on what a miracle this precious lifetime is, we are walking in the kingdom of heaven, Thầy said. Never a day went by that he was not walking in the kingdom of God.

Because of the brain injury, I was unable to fall into my old habits of skepticism and cynicism; I just followed directions. I focused on this amazing world with each step, and at the end of the walk I felt wonderful. I realized that where I chose to place my mind determined my experience. I had a choice! It was truly a miracle of mindfulness.

At the same retreat, Thầy was working with Vietnam veterans to help them heal from the war. One veteran asked Thầy why he did not hate American soldiers after what they had done to his country. Thầy immediately answered that nobody ever wins a war; everyone loses. Hostilities may end, but the pain and suffering inflicted on people and the humiliation of those who were defeated just sow seeds for the next war. Soldiers, Thầy said, are the hands of the body of humanity. They are sent into the fire, but the whole body feels the pain. I was stunned by the depth of his insights.

I had come of age during the Vietnam War and was active in the peace movement. I witnessed the dualistic conflicts within this peace movement that created yet another war. We were right, those causing the war were wrong. We were good, those causing the war were bad. This just created more conflict. It was very ineffective and unskillful.

Witnessing Thầy in dialogue with the veterans and seeing his unconditional love, acceptance, and compassion was very inspiring. It was clear that he knew something I also needed to understand. I had no idea how a person who was harmed could do anything but criticize, judge, blame, and hate those who had harmed them. But in Thầy I saw compassion with my own eyes.

As his student, I began to experience the fruits of the practice. With gentle diligence over time I learned to stop, breathe, and look deeply in order to understand the suffering of those who cause suffering. This allowed me to understand and to try to find ways to help, rather than to criticize, blame, and want to punish.

What I experienced was freedom. That is what I saw in Thầy at that first retreat. He was not caught in hatred and anger or holding onto resentment. He was free. After getting a small taste of that freedom, all I wanted to do was look at all the aspects of my life that I could change to become even freer and happier.

I have been living with stage four metastatic cancer for the last twelve years. Receiving the diagnosis, I had no idea what lay ahead. *I have limited minutes to live*, I thought. *How many do I want to spend in fear and speculation?* The answer was zero. I have spent very few moments worrying about the future. Instead I practice saying to myself, "I don't know," and I do my best to enjoy every moment—with my husband and our Sangha, watching the hummingbirds and butterflies visit the flowers we planted for them, and witnessing the wonders of life.

Joanne Friday died on January 20, 2021. As a dharma teacher in Thầy's tradition, Joanne embodied the "miracle of this precious lifetime" that she recounts here. Joanne lived in the United States, working as a crisis counselor, teacher, and visual artist first, then in retirement leading meditation retreats for Sanghas and groups throughout the Northeast. She was ordained into the Order of Interbeing in 1999, became a dharma teacher in 2003, and was the guiding dharma teacher for seven Sanghas comprising the Rhode Island Community of Mindfulness. One of her favorites was the Generations Sangha, which brings Thầy's teachings to children and their parents. She also served as an Associate Chaplain at the University of Rhode Island. Joanne said that her dharma name, True Joy of Giving, reflected her understanding that Thầy and the Buddha have given us the gift of this beautiful path. Being able to share the path with others was her greatest joy. Joanne contributed chapters to two books by Thích Nhất Hạnh—*Reconciliation: Healing the Inner Child* and *Friends on the Path: Living Spiritual Communities*.

A Tiny but Perfect Cloud

by Jared Bibler

IN THE LATE SUMMER OF 2012, my wife Hulda and I
decide to make a change after some years of struggle. It is a
scary undertaking for us, but it also is a good time for tran-
sition. Hulda has just finished her degree, I have completed
a number of huge projects at work, and we have not yet
started a family. After talking for years about moving to
Switzerland to seek a better life, we are at last putting the
plan into action. We will do it in two phases: in phase one,
she will stay behind and keep her job and our apartment,
just in case. I will move ahead to Zürich; once I find a new
job and a new apartment, she can join me.

I leave Reykjavík by car in early September, just days
before the first serious winter storm hits. I drive 750 kilometers around the northern half of Iceland to get to Seyðis-
fjörður, the departure harbor for the Norrøna ferry. It is
nearly four days at sea, and then, once in Denmark, I must
drive another 1,500 kilometers south across Germany to
get to Switzerland. I have laid my groundwork well: within
a few weeks of arriving, I have a nice job offer that is a step
up in my career. I start the new job a few weeks after that.

In a brand-new place where I need to learn a new language and miss having my wife by my side, I am often very lonely. I find a small room to rent in a nice house, and my new job is very challenging. I spend long hours at the office. I tell Hulda she can come right away, but her boss will not say exactly when he will release her from her employment contract. In addition to taking care of closing up our old life in Iceland, Hulda may have to continue her job for up to three more months. We are frustrated, but we keep hoping.

For many years, I had been drawn to Thích Nhất Hạnh's teachings; I even read his book about love when I was much younger. Now, alone in Zurich, I stumble across an online announcement that his dharma talks are being released as podcasts. The news is like a glimpse of cool water in my lonely desert. I download and listen right away. My first podcast is even in English and German, the language I happen to be trying to learn. Thầy pauses after each sentence to let his soft-spoken translator shape the message into German.

Right away, I find a new way to look at life. New episodes are coming out every few days, and they are wonderful; I listen to each one. I try a little walking meditation on the way home one night in my new Swiss town, and the experience is profound. The world of the present moment feels more vivid: I really see the old cobblestones of the street and the soft Christmas lights above for the first time. I listen to a podcast episode every day on the train, and then I listen again later when I am falling asleep. The words begin to transform me. I start to feel peaceful despite the stress of being in a new country, starting a new job, and experiencing lonely weekends.

Hulda's boss makes her work until the final hour of the very last day of her contract, so we end up spending five long months apart. At last, we are reunited in our new country, and we move into a lovely new apartment together a week later. As we are falling asleep one night, I play her some snippets from the podcast. To my surprise, she immediately takes to it. She asks to hear it again a few evenings later. She especially loves to listen to the story of the cloud that never dies, the cloud that becomes a river or a lake and waves to us from its new form.

One sunny Saturday afternoon, a few months after Hulda arrived and we began our new life together, my wife suffers a fatal accident. There is no way to save her; she dies instantly.

I drive home, numb and shocked, and call her family in Iceland. Some friends come over to comfort me. I lie alone in bed late at night, trying to fall asleep, but I experience a type and level of emotion I haven't yet faced in my life. Realizing what I need to do, I find the podcast and listen to Thầy speaking about the cloud. With his peaceful and reassuring voice, everything clicks: in that moment, I feel the deep truth that Hulda has not disappeared, but continued. I am even able to smile about it a little bit. At last, I can get to sleep and experience a few peaceful hours.

The next morning, I sit outside in the sun and try for the first time in years to practice sitting meditation. The lavender plants on my balcony seem to be waving to me in the breeze. I feel connected to my wife even though she isn't here in a physical form. I can sense that she is here in other forms.

A few weeks later, as I am thinking of Hulda, I see a single, tiny-but-perfect cloud in the otherwise clear evening sky.

Step by step, I work to rebuild my life. I find a compassionate therapist who helps me take care of myself through the first difficult months. I practice more meditation, begin to journal, and take better care of my body. I become drawn to the beautiful nature all around me in Switzerland. I adopt one of Hulda's passions as my own: although I have never sung in my life, I join a local men's choir. There I meet two other widowers who take me under their wing. I read deeply about grief and loss. And always in the background is Thầy's soft voice.

I listen to each new dharma talk as it comes out, many of them two or three times. Although Thầy often repeats the same simple messages, I experience a new kind of wisdom in his gentle voice.

The following summer I make the two-day drive to Plum Village, Thầy's retreat center in France, for the first time. When the monks and nuns chant to Avalokitesvara, a woman two rows in front of me begins to weep gently. Her friend moves to comfort her, placing an arm across her back. Then I hear someone else behind me start to cry. All at once it is my turn too. My body shakes with tears of deep sorrow as the movie of the day Hulda died plays over and over in my head. Alone at home I have cried this way many times, but now it is as if the chanting monastics, led by Thầy, are somehow lifting the sorrow from me.

It feels as though a great bodhisattva is in the room with us, listening to our suffering. Someone can hear my deep grief. I begin, in these moments, to feel healed and transformed. I share the story of Hulda with my dharma family, and they ask to hear more about her. Two evenings later, they smile as I show photos and tell them about our life together. I am no longer alone in my sorrow.

That week, I have the great honor to walk side by side with Thầy through the orchards of New Hamlet. For a few steps, it feels as if it is only the two of us walking, followed by hundreds of fellow travelers under the bright Aquitaine sky.

Jared Bibler lives in Switzerland and practices with the Sangha des Herzens in Zürich and with a virtual Sangha he created, Sangha S33. He feels closer to his dharma name, Rising Sun of the Heart, which he received in Plum Village in 2016, than to his birth name. It brings him great happiness and serves as both inspiration and aspiration. Jared is a consultant in investigations and sustainable finance with his own consulting firm, Katla AG. As one of the first investigators to examine Iceland's financial crash of 2008, Jared tells the story of how massive financial crime led to the collapse of Iceland's economy in his book, *Iceland's Secret*.

Unwrapping My Present

by Alejandro Cerda

I WAS MARRIED TO A WONDERFUL woman with beautiful eyes that could see beyond things. She had a tireless determination to achieve what she wanted. She was tender, spontaneous, and full of smiles. Before we got married, we were together for five years and went through challenging situations that strengthened our commitment as a couple. We had to figure out together how to maintain an apartment while she studied and worked. In addition, we lived more than 10,000 kilometers apart for a year and had to nourish our relationship by emails and phone calls.

We really enjoyed each other's company and worked as a team: we did housework together, made our own meals due to our low budget, and made plans for her graduation and job search. But our marriage began on the shaky foundation of unexplored volition—we hadn't looked closely at what each of us desired. Though our intentions were good, we didn't know how to handle our relationship or how to make ourselves happy. I was emotionally illiterate and didn't know how to ask for help, for a hug, or for cheering words when I was depressed or overwhelmed. I did not know how to practice loving speech and deep listening.

My wife and I acquired a lot of debt together while trying to achieve goals we thought would make us happy. Instead, they created a pressure that eventually crushed our relationship. We could not stay together; we didn't have the clarity to realize that we had each other, and that this was the only thing that really mattered.

Our difficulty in loving took us to a very exhausting and sad stage. We divorced after two and a half years, and the process for me was long, difficult, and painful—I had a very strong attachment to my wife. During the first months of our separation, craving, anger, despair, and confusion were my daily thoughts and nourishment. Whether it was daytime or nighttime, my mind wandered; I lived in depression and anxiety all the time. I felt an excruciating pressure, as if something or someone was holding a boulder on my chest and preventing me from breathing.

My pain came not just from the depression of not wanting to accept that my marriage was over, but also from day-to-day anxiety brought on by certain decisions my ex-wife made for her own well-being after our separation. Wounded and immature, I reacted inappropriately, childishly, and I behaved hurtfully towards the person I had once sworn to love throughout my life. Later, I understood that it was not my ex-wife who hurt me. It was I who, unable to recognize my own suffering, blamed her instead of working on myself.

One afternoon during these difficult days, I was looking for a movie that could distract my mind and allow me to avoid being angry, at least for a few minutes. While watching TV, I came across a movie called *Walk with Me*. It was about life in a monastery called Plum Village, founded in France by a monk named Thích Nhất Hạnh. I had never heard his name, so I decided to start watching.

From the very first scene, the movie caught my attention. It was the first time I learned about Thầy. During the movie, a song called "Namo Avalokitesvara" was performed by a group of monastics. Listening to this song, sung in a language I did not even understand, I started to feel a great peace. I began to cry in a way I had never imagined that I could cry. This song in some way helped me to stop and to embrace my fears, my hate, and my anxiety. I felt very relieved.

When the movie ended, I realized that my heart was tired of feeling so much anger, and a feeling of happiness suddenly sprouted there. As Thầy says, "Once we recognize our suffering, we start to feel relieved." I started to read Thầy's teachings and was determined to attend a retreat. I was lucky to attend the 2018 New Year's retreat at Deer Park, a monastery established by Thầy in Escondido, California.

The first day of the retreat, a monk named Thầy Phap Hai welcomed us with these three words: "Unwrap your present." He explained it was a metaphor. When we remove the layers of depression that make us live in the past and remove the layers of anxiety that make us live in the future, what remains is our "present." That is our gift, the only place where we can be happy. At that moment, the pain I had in my chest, pain that I had been carrying for months, disappeared.

After that trip to Deer Park, one question prowled my mind. What would have happened if I had known Thầy's teachings before my divorce? Maybe I would still be married. I was fixated on this idea for a couple of weeks before I found the answer in Thầy's teachings—the concept of manifestation. "This is what Buddha taught: when conditions are sufficient, things manifest. When conditions are no longer sufficient, things withdraw. They wait until the moment is right for them to manifest again."

I smiled when I read this, and it made me feel relieved, motivated, and happy to continue my life and to wish my ex-wife the best. I discovered that I have the responsibility and the opportunity to be a better human being now, in the present moment. Thầy's teachings showed me a way to understand my suffering and to feel compassion instead of guilty toward my unwholesome feelings. I understood that this suffering is not merely mine but also my ancestors'.

Because of Thích Nhất Hạnh, I now know that happiness comes from practicing compassion—not just for others, or just for what I think or do today, but also compassion for myself, for my past, and for the ways that I have hurt people I love because of my wrong perceptions.

Alejandro Cerda lives in México and started a small but cozy Sangha with close friends called Wake Up San Luis Potosí. He received a lot of support, encouragement, and confidence to take this small but lovely step. The group is learning with love and the best of intentions to embrace suffering under the shelter of Thầy's teachings. Alejandro believes his dharma name, Refuge of the Heart, captures the value he has found in discovering this spiritual path, which has offered a roadmap for healing and for transforming his sorrow after his divorce.

Practicing Happiness
in the Face of Death

by Anne von der Lühe

THE FIRST TIME I WAS DIAGNOSED with cancer, I did not know that one day I would be careening down a snowy hill on a sled, flanked by brown-robed Vietnamese monks and nuns rejoicing in rudimentary German. Neither did I imagine myself stuck at home, jobless and alone, wondering how I would survive with my children away in college and my husband running off with another woman. Yet both of these experiences would bring me to the spaciousness with which I greeted my second, more deadly cancer diagnosis fourteen years after the first.

At the age of forty-two, I learned I had breast cancer. I thought I might die and that I would die alone. At that time I did not know anything about interbeing, the interconnectedness of all phenomena and all beings. My thoughts made me very sad and filled me with fear. I had a strong bodily sensation of the ground being taken from under my feet. My sense of security, my trust in life, and my sense of connection suddenly vanished from my physical experience of myself, my feelings, and my thoughts.

Driving down the road one day, I heard a radio program about the Vietnamese Zen master Thích Nhất Hạnh, who had opened a practice center in Germany. Retreats were planned there for the coming summer. Although I knew nothing about Buddhism or Vietnamese culture, I had the feeling that this information would change my life. Not knowing what to expect at a Zen center, I was afraid of making all sorts of embarrassing mistakes. On the other hand, I had nothing holding me down—no job, no family obligations—and a retreat seemed like the right way to spend what turned out to be the next two years of my life.

The European Institute for Applied Buddhism (EIAB) in Waldbröl was one of several retreat centers Thầy created around the world to facilitate the study and practice of mindfulness. As a resident there, I put my professional skills to use by teaching German to the Vietnamese sisters and brothers, who were very eager to learn, and by translating various documents and dharma talks to help grow the community. I taught the monks and nuns a new language, and they taught me a new way to see the world and my place in it. I started with one sentence: "I am aware that being happy comes from my inner attitude and does not depend on external circumstances." The monastics taught me to focus on living happily in the present moment by remembering that I already have more than enough conditions to be happy. My days at the EIAB presented many ways to work on this inner attitude—pausing when the mindfulness bell sounded every fifteen minutes, singing songs before walking meditation, and reciting Thầy's gathas, short verses posted everywhere to remind me of my practice.

I was building a new family, a Sangha of monastic sisters and brothers who in both gentle and lively ways helped me realize that I had all the conditions within myself to be happy. They held my hand when my tears flowed and helped me transform tremendous sadness. We shared many happy moments—gentle smiles; beautiful, calm walks in the forest; lively moments playing ball together; wild adventures sledding down the hill in the apple orchard. These simple, daily practices and a deeper study of the Five Mindfulness Trainings, which teach us how to live life more joyfully, taught me to dwell increasingly in the present moment. Though I had arrived at the EIAB with a strong habit energy of needing to serve and contribute, I came to understand what my brothers and sisters told me time and again: Anne, you don't need to do anything. Being, not doing, is your contribution to Sangha life.

Living and practicing at the EIAB, I focused on mindfulness skills—simply trying to see things as they are and checking if I can be completely open to whatever physical feeling or mental formation arises. When I was ordained as a member of the Order of Interbeing, Thầy's community of people committed to mindfulness and compassionate action in society, I received the dharma name True Inclusiveness of the Ocean. There is a teaching of the Buddha that if you pour a handful of salt into a glass full of water, the water will be undrinkable. When you pour a handful of salt into the ocean, however, the water is not affected in any substantial way. I did not know how essential such a profound understanding of being present would be for my life. I became as spacious and open as the ocean.

Seven years later, that is how I received the news that I had metastatic pancreatic cancer. The cancer had already spread to my liver, and my situation was much direr than my first diagnosis had been. Hearing this news, I was able to accept it without resistance. In my mind I felt strong like the mountains and firm like the earth. I was calm, I felt room inside, and I was not crowded by despair or uneasiness. I was open like the ocean.

Now I experienced first-hand what I had learned: if you can accept ill health in your body, you suffer much less. I thought to myself, *That is it, and there is nothing else to do but breathe.*

The night following the diagnosis, I lay awake for a while. I recalled how I had been confronted with death fourteen years earlier, and how alone I had felt then. At that time, I had thought to myself, *If I die, I am completely alone; I have to undertake this journey all by myself.* This time, after years of studying and practicing Thầy's teachings, was different. In just the same way that I felt the soft, firm bed on which I was lying in the darkness, I also felt union with all living creatures, with mother earth, with my loved ones, and in particular with my Sangha. In my mind's eye I saw my mother, my children, and my partner. Alongside them I saw my beloved teachers and dharma sisters and brothers to whom I felt so closely bound through our journey on the same path, our shared practice, and the deep experience of interbeing.

I experience every day that when the thought of death is absent, fear is also absent: no death, no fear. This doesn't mean that I deny my own mortality. I am aware of it every moment. This is precisely what makes life so beautiful.

I don't tell myself stories about how dramatic my situation is. I don't go looking for information on the internet; that action is not wholesome or helpful for me. Instead, I have complete trust in my doctor, who is a very competent and compassionate person. In this moment, I am fully aware that death is only a thought. One day this body will stop breathing, this heart will beat its final beat. But that is not now; in this moment I have all the conditions necessary to live a truly wonderful life.

Anne von der Lühe lives in Germany and practices with the Fourfold Sangha in Waldbröl and the Clouds and Sunshine Sangha in Cologne. Ordained as a member of the Order of Interbeing in 2012, she was given the dharma name True Inclusiveness of the Ocean. Anne says this name helps her let go of all prejudice and judgment and to see and accept phenomena as they are. In her professional life, she was a high school teacher of German, French, and Spanish and contributed mindfulness in schools research to Ulrich Pfeifer-Schaupp's book, *Leben mit dem Herzen eines Buddhas*. Anne spent several years in Africa before settling in Cologne.

PART 7

Being Here Now:
The Wonders of the
Present Moment

Finding Balance in a Wooden Canoe

by María Victoria Rivera-Paez
and Nicolás Bermúdez Vélez

IN THE MID-1990S, as a newlywed couple, we lived and worked in the Colombian Amazon. We travelled by wooden canoe to join family groups gathering wild fruit and gardening in small clearings in the rainforest. As anthropologists, we wanted to build a bridge between Indigenous communities and the Western world, to raise awareness of Indigenous ways of life as a source of insight into how to care for Mother Earth. We spent about eight months each year staying in malokas, communal long-houses, and sharing the local people's everyday lives and rituals.

Life in the rainforest was challenging, with many physical risks. We had no electricity, running water, motor vehicles, or any of the comforts of the city life we were used to. We knew we had a chance to learn to live with simplicity and austerity and to enjoy the wonders of life through very close contact with nature's elements and forces. But we wondered: Could we also add parenthood and still maintain the focus we needed for our work in this strange, often hostile environment?

When a close friend arrived one day from a trip to the United Kingdom carrying one of Thích Nhất Hạnh's books, we discovered a new teacher, a kindred spirit who could help us celebrate our connection to the Earth and enjoy the wonders of life at every moment, no matter where we were or what we were doing.

Thầy talks about a friend who was troubled by having to divide his time between his work, his personal life, and taking care of his son. Thầy explained to his friend that he didn't have to divide his time, since he could choose to see the time he spent with his son as his own time, as time for himself. This opened our eyes to the wonderful possibility of understanding and enriching our own experience of parenthood. The key was now right in front of us: the side-by-side examples of our Indigenous hosts and Thầy's teachings.

We discovered that our work with communities along the river made it easy to be there as a family. Our three young children, Irene, Silvia, and Elena, were able to play around us and to get involved in everything we did, whether it was walking through the forest, planting, weeding, and harvesting in the gardens, navigating along the river, or visiting people's houses for local meetings. Our daughters were usually thrilled when the time came for ritual dances; together with other children, they would help the household prepare to receive many guests, and they wholeheartedly enjoyed the communal feast, which would last three days and nights.

As a young family, we spent time daily bathing in the clear stream near the Amazonian community where we lived. We washed our clothes together while admiring butterflies and tiny fish that came to lick our skin. The girls naturally did their part while also playing around and learning to swim freely with their peers. They walked with mindful steps and concentration so as not to tread on snakes, insects, or thorns on the way. They were proud to carry a basket with wild fruit along a forest trail and then to carefully use large knives to help peel and grate the manioc back in the long-house.

Learning basic math happened while traveling for hours on a wooden canoe along the river between communities, when we stopped on sandy banks to collect beautiful pebbles and classify their shapes, colors, sizes, and series. We also loved the game of counting the pairs of macaws that flew in flocks overhead every now and then and imitating their shrieks, which resounded in the immensity of the surrounding rainforest. There was so much fun in being there together, in discovering the wonders of life all around us, in learning how to name things in the local languages, and in trying to live with the skills and wisdom of our Indigenous hosts.

This was very different from our life back in Bogotá, where we spent the rest of the year writing up reports on our work and doing administrative tasks to help raise funds and educate the public about respecting biocultural diversity. During these phases, we had to separate from our children during the day. At the beginning they went to daycare, later to school. Adapting and getting used to being together for only a little while in the morning and then again later in the evening was a challenge.

Often, we would come home to find our kids watching TV, chewing gum, or eating junk food with their cousins while their grandmothers or aunts were in charge. As devoted parents, it was a difficult scene for us to accept. Our daughters were confused by their grandmothers rejecting their common Amazonian etiquette, such as eating with their hands, running barefoot all day long, and spitting on the floor.

Through meditation, we learned to let go of our fixed ideas about proper upbringing without feeling guilty or being careless. Sometimes strong emotions arose, like anger or impatience or jealousy, and it wasn't easy to understand what was going on inside each of us. When harsh words or yelling came up to express resentment about our late arrival after work, we practiced stopping to close our eyes and breathe five or ten times together as a family before saying anything else. Then we would try to name what we felt behind or under the rude behavior and where it was in the body. We all saw that we can talk peacefully and that emotions come and go; we need not see them as something bigger than ourselves. Some years later, we learned Thầy's practice of Beginning Anew, a reconciliation process that became one of our favorite ways to heal the unskillful moments we encountered in our family.

Thầy's teachings helped us build a bridge between our life in the city and our life in the Amazon by creating new agreements about caring for each other and enjoying our togetherness in the present moment. These agreements slowly became part of our family's special culture. We sang mindfulness songs from the heart while driving in the car and sang our gratitude to Mother Earth for the food on our table every day. With shared awe for the wonders of life, we made a point of respecting the life of animals, plants, and minerals and asking for permission to take something from nature. In this way, we continued the reverence and compassion we learned in the rainforest.

Eventually, we built a home in the Andean village of Sopó, outside of Bogotá. Following Thầy's counsel, we set up a special sacred space in our bedroom where we lit a candle and incense before practice sitting meditation every day. At first, our daughters found this boring and got impatient, but in time they found solace in the serene atmosphere of our special breathing space and began to feel the benefit of what they had scorned. Soon they were coming close to quietly sit next to us, listen to the silence, and feel the rhythm of our mindful breathing. Sometimes they brought a cushion of their own to sit for a short while and share calm, healing energy.

With each child we made a collection of special pebbles, which they kept in a special bag or box. With these pebbles we practiced Pebble Meditation to cultivate their own beauty, freshness, solidity, and freedom. The girls learned to treasure their pebbles and would carry or hold them during difficult times. We also gave sets of four beautiful pebbles to our kids' cousins and friends and taught them to practice as well. It was marvelous to learn from Thầy how to offer children and ourselves new practices to find a way back home, so that we could be ourselves as the best way to be beautiful.

In 2014, Plum Village monastics visited Colombia. It was wonderful to participate in a workshop with them and to practice Tangerine Meditation in a big hall, peeling and mindfully eating tangerines with 120 other practitioners. This inspired us to join and support the new Open

Dharma Door Sangha in Bogotá, where we as a family could share our practice with others. During this Sangha-building period, we watched our daughters grow into young adults in whose personal lives the teachings continue to be important. They incorporate different practices of mindfulness from the Plum village tradition into their work lives. They have chosen to become members of our Sangha on their own and participate in many of the weekly meditation sessions, Days of Mindfulness, and retreats, drawing other young people in with them.

María Victoria Rivera-Paez and *Nicolás Bermúdez Vélez* live on a small farm in Colombia, where they practice with two Sanghas that they co-founded—the Open Dharma Door in Bogotá and the Colombian Sangha in Bogotá and Medellín. They facilitate meetings and activities for the online Sangha de las Americas, a Spanish-speaking group that includes people in Colombia, Ecuador, Chile, Argentina, México, and Puerto Rico. María Victoria's dharma name, True Direction of Love, reminds her that now she has a path to live in fearless connection with love and interbeing as Thầy's continuation and a beautiful source of love. Nicolás's dharma name, True Direction of Loyalty, offers him a powerful reminder to show up daily to the essence of his aspiration, which is to be true to himself, to his loved ones, and to the Sangha. María and Nicolás were ordained into the Order of Interbeing in 2022, and they have contributed articles to the *Mindfulness Bell* magazine.

What Is Eating Me

by Coralee Hicks

WHEN I FIRST READ Thích Nhất Hạnh's *Savor: Mindful Eating, Mindful Life*, I was like the sunbaked earth longing for a soaking rain to bring me back to myself. Having stopped drinking alcohol in 1984, I was a person in recovery, practicing diligently. But despite my long exposure to Buddhist philosophy, I had not incorporated mindfulness into my recovery tool box.

My alcoholic story is common. Suffice it to say I came from a family where emotions were suppressed and thoughts were clouded by drink. As a child, I promised myself I would never abuse my body in such a manner. I wish I had listened more carefully to that child.

Growing up in the Pacific Northwest, the natural beauty, mists, fogs, and gentle rains, which people now come to visit from all parts of the world, were part of my daily experience. I was surrounded by many Buddhists as well as by images of the Buddha, and I walked often through the Japanese Garden designed by Masters Kiyoshi Inoshita, Juki Iida, and their team. I had a doorway through which I could eventually step into the world of mindfulness.

Before I could do that, there were a few rivers of challenge that I had to bridge. First, how could I honor my values during the US involvement in the Vietnam War? I had always been a peace advocate, as was my fiancé. While at the University of Washington during the troop buildup between 1965 and 1968, we discussed leaving the country to avoid killing. Ultimately, we made the decision to stay and accept what was to come. My fiancé was drafted into the Air Force and landed in Vietnam a week after the Tet Offensive in 1968. A year later, we married, and I joined him at the US military base on Okinawa.

We were warriors fighting on two fronts as we grappled with questions that shook us to the core. What was our responsibility? Duty to country, even when we believed our country was wrong? Or duty to the world, duty to seek a more compassionate way? We kept these conversations off base, knowing we could lose our security clearance if others judged that our talk of peace made us the enemy. Fear dominated. There was no peace, and we dulled our minds with drugs and alcohol.

The next river that I had to ford was my anger. It flowed as steadily and slowly as molten lava, full of resentment about growing up in a time of limited and constraining roles for women in society. I was never good enough for heaven or smart enough to stay out of hell. My anger became a sullen lake inside that threatened my harmony. It kept me always off balance and soured my relationship with my husband. Despite a year of counseling, we decided to end our marriage. Released from our marriage vows, we continued as loving friends until his death in 1997.

The final river for me to negotiate was the sorrow of my disability. Today, I am severely hard of hearing. This loss built slowly, progressing from losing the sound of a clock ticking and then a cat's purr to missing out on normal conversation. I had to change careers as I moved from the world of sound to the world of silence. Now I no longer hear the rain, whether it makes a gentle song or a torrential downpour. How can I be a compassionate listener if I cannot hear?

Within these challenges that life threw my way, I eventually accomplished a major victory: not drinking alcohol. Yet my cravings were like a bottomless well that never could be filled. In peril of looking for a more serious substance to abuse, I tried to comfort myself with food instead. I wasn't using illegal drugs, harming my family by gambling, or seeking comfort in false intimacy. I was on the track of recovery, right?

Wrong. After ten years of abstaining from alcohol, I had gained more than a hundred pounds. Guilt, shame, and self-hatred engulfed me.

Thầy wrote in *Savor*: "We must learn how to make friends with our hardships and challenges. They are there to help us; they are natural opportunities for deeper understanding and transformation, bringing us more joy and peace as we learn to work with them."

Reading that book felt like having a conversation with a loving sage who knew how to lift me from the torrential rivers I had been traversing. Thầy offered a guide and concrete strategies for making peace with food and creating a happier life. He did not use fear as a tactic to encourage change, as is typical in the weight-loss industry. Rather than prescribing a restricted meal plan, he encouraged a plant-based diet. For the first time, weight management was not a challenge for me. Instead, I had an opportunity for transformation.

While visiting a local mindfulness center that follows the Plum Village tradition, I noticed that very few of the people were overweight. *There must be something to this*, I thought, and began to follow the Five Mindfulness Trainings, which are guidelines to live life with less suffering and more joy. Originating from the Buddha, these trainings were adapted by Thích Nhất Hạnh and his community for our modern times.

The first training emphasizes reverence for life and not killing. "Aware of the suffering caused by the destruction of life, I am committed to cultivating the insight of interbeing and compassion and learning ways to protect the lives of people, animals, plants, and minerals."

It occurred to me one day that "people" meant not killing myself either. I decided to change what I was eating and moved towards a plant-based diet. After studying the Fifth Mindfulness Training, which focuses on consuming in a way that promotes nourishment and healing, I realized that some foods created cravings. If I ate refined sugar, I wanted more. So step one was to stop drinking sweetened iced tea. Next, I stopped buying packaged cereals. Today, if sugar is an ingredient in an American recipe I'm using, I reduce the amount by half.

After a while, I started to explore what a plant-based diet meant to someone raised in the West and wondered why the vegetarian food industry tries to imitate animal protein. Why not study cuisines of other countries that have already developed wonderful vegetarian recipes? I studied food blogs from México, China, Central Asia, and India, and when something looked interesting, I made it. I also watched videos of cooking techniques for various cuisines, and I learned that spices are much more tasty than salt. A new world opened to me.

Living in today and leaving yesterday behind, while holding gentle aspirations for the future, is my daily intention. Am I always mindful, especially concerning food? Of course not. There are mornings I feel an overwhelming sense of *I don't want to do this!* while sitting on my meditation cushion. In these moments, I breathe and look deeper. I am aware of my age, past seventy. I am aware that I have several chronic diseases, due in part to overeating and in part to genetic history, that demand daily attention. However, if my feelings of resistance become stronger, I am also aware that I can take a day off from all of it—the planning, the meal prep, the cooking. This usually shifts my energy. If negative voices grow stronger, I look into what is eating me rather than what I am eating.

Soothing has become a watchword for me. When I become aware of mounting anxiety, I take a day to prepare a meal as if Thầy were in my kitchen guiding me. First, I sit. I breathe, do a mind-body check, breathe, and welcome the present. Knowing the meal preparation requires performing several tasks simultaneously, I go over the steps before gathering the ingredients. As I look at the *mise en place*, I consider the farmers who grew the food and the workers who harvested the food. I thank them for their labor. Aware that workers in factories are often operating in hazardous situations, I send thoughts of well-being towards them. I thank the plants and animals that gave their lives so I might live.

The cooking itself becomes a flow of scents and flavors as I stir, check, and patiently wait. Timers that ring are treated as invited mindfulness bells. Cooking is generous; pausing a moment to focus on the present will not burn the soup. Setting a table for one, I silently say the Five Contemplations before my meal:

- ◎ This food is a gift of the earth, the sky, numerous living beings, and much hard and loving work.

- ◎ May we eat with mindfulness and gratitude so as to be worthy to receive this food.

- ◎ May we recognize and transform unwholesome mental formations, especially our greed, and learn to eat with moderation.

- ◎ May we keep our compassion alive by eating in such a way that reduces the suffering of living beings, stops contributing to climate change, and heals and preserves our precious planet.

- ◎ We accept this food so that we may nurture our brotherhood and sisterhood, build our Sangha, and nourish our ideal of serving all living beings.

I picture the monks and nuns in Thầy's monasteries sharing these exact contemplations before a meal. Breathing in, I am connected to others eating in the same manner. Breathing out, I am grateful for a spiritual connection that can be felt even when I am alone.

Coralee Hicks lives in the United States and practices with the Florida Community of Mindfulness in Tampa. Her dharma name, Source of Freedom and Ease, serves as a reminder for her to let go and release herself of anxiety. She jokingly calls herself a shortened version: Free. Coralee, who lived for several years in Asia before settling in Florida, has two daughters and two grandchildren.

Thank You for Being Late

by Nicole Dunn

I WAS WAITING.

And waiting.

My husband Mike was due to pick me up in our one shared vehicle: a trusty old Ford Econoline van, which we affectionately called Humphrey. I was twenty-two years old; we lived in the van in a Philadelphia suburb and were saving money to move back to Missoula, Montana, where we had met and married. I was a preschool teacher, and Mike was working at U-Haul. Our normal routine involved Mike dropping me off at work in the morning and me walking down the road to the library when I finished with work so that Mike could pick me up there when he was done with his shift.

On this evening, I was looking forward to our next stop: meditating with our Sangha. Although we had only been attending the weekly group for a short time, I had quickly taken to it; I found it refreshing and grounding.

As pick-up time drew closer, I went outside to wait for Mike, but ten minutes went by with no sign of him. I began to wonder what time it was, so I went into the library to check. Since my idea of being on time is arriving ten minutes early, I started to feel irritated as the clock continued to tick. I especially didn't want to be late to meditation, which offered me a sense of stability and ease that I carried with me throughout the week.

Back outside, I anxiously scanned the road for any sign of Humphrey. After ten more minutes and another check of the clock, I proceeded to get very impatient—I went from irritated to frustrated. I paced back and forth along the sidewalk, thinking to myself, *Where the heck is he? This is ridiculous!* Another ten minutes, back inside for another time check, and my frustration was now fuming anger. I stormed outside again, muttering profanities to myself as I paced rapidly and kept a militant eye on the road.

In the midst of my internal and external fuming, I sat down on a bench and exhaled heavily in exasperation as I slumped against the wooden slats. I tilted my head back until my face pointed upwards to the sky. It was then that I received a message, as though it were etched in the clouds overhead: just enjoy me.

Those words resonated loud and gentle and clear. The present moment had sent me a message. In that instant, I was aware of how embittered I had become while waiting. How tense my body and mind were. I saw how futile all my pacing and checking of the time and angry mutterings were—though it seems painfully clear to me now, I realized that my ranting and raving wasn't going to make Mike arrive any sooner. During my thirty-minute escalation, I had no idea how stressed out and irrational I had become. On the bench, I was able to apply the teachings I had only recently started learning from Thích Nhất Hạnh. With the words "just enjoy me," the light of mindfulness shone through my thick fog of anger.

I got up from the bench and suddenly realized what a beautiful spring day it was. The sky was magnificently blue, the afternoon sun warm and welcoming. I practiced slow walking meditation in the same space where a few minutes before I had been madly pacing. I admired the budding trees and green grass. I shifted my gaze away from anxiously watching the road to my immediate surroundings, and I got in touch with my breath. These were things I'd been learning through Thầy's books and at our Sangha; on this day, instead of me being with the Sangha in the meditation hall, the Sangha was there with me outside of the library.

Once I was calm, I could look more deeply into why Mike might be late. It was highly unlikely that he had voluntarily chosen not to pick me up on time. I saw clearly that he was probably helping a customer and unable to clock out as scheduled. As Thầy teaches, I stopped waiting for him to arrive and practiced instead to arrive myself, in the here and the now. I let myself enjoy the day, and that truly made all the difference. The time I had spent waiting felt like an exhausting, agonizing eternity, even though it had only been thirty minutes. The same amount of time spent enjoying the present moment was refreshing and energizing.

When Mike finally arrived, much too late to go to meditation, I greeted him with a smile and said: "Thank you for being late." And I meant it. I was very aware that, without the transformation his lateness precipitated, my first words would have been different and the evening would have been ruined by my anger-fueled words and actions.

Nicole Dunn lives in the United States and practices with the Be Here Now Sangha, which she founded in Missoula, Montana in 2002. She was ordained into the Order of Interbeing in 2007 and given the dharma name True Wonderful Flower. Nicole writes a column called "Mindfulness Matters" for *Montana Woman Magazine*. She is an active blogger, produced the spoken word album *Bird on a Wire*, and is working on a book project called *Get Ur Joy On*. She has also been a hospice volunteer for more than twenty years. Nicole's greatest happiness is in being a Sangha builder, and she and her husband Mike are working on starting a small, rustic mindfulness practice center in western Montana called Empty Mountain.

Acknowledgments

AS MY BIGGEST FAN, my mom supported me in doing all that I wanted, whether it was trekking from Germany to Finland in my twenties, starting my own business, or writing this book. She had a fierce confidence in me that provided a bridge during times when I myself had none. When she learned I was Buddhist, her Christian heart stayed open and curious until she eventually understood that our paths merged. Having lost her in the last year of editing this book, I am so grateful for her presence in my life.

She would be proud of this book, as would my dad, who was inherently more like a Buddha than me or anyone in the family. Silently, he would sit under a shade tree enjoying the birds and watching the sky change. We once traveled to Vietnam together; Dad wanted to return to the country he fell in love with as a soldier, and we visited Thích Nhất Hạnh's root temple in Hue. It was a magical moment for us, full of appreciation for life's unexpected coincidences. Never, we mused, could we have imagined that forty years later Dad would see Vietnam through the eyes of his daughter and a Vietnamese Buddhist monk. Thank you, Mom and Dad, for your influence and your unyielding love. This book would not exist without it.

I am also grateful for Mary, my co-editor, who leaned into my book idea with such commitment and care that she made it her own and developed deep connections with many of the writers as a midwife of their stories. This book, thanks to your wisdom and love, is now outstanding.

Thank you to my partner, Colleen, and my daughter, Nicole, for giving me the space and time to massage this book these last few years. I love you both. And to everyone else who touched my life along the way: your presence mattered.

—JEANINE

WITHOUT THESE PEOPLE, I might still be wandering around in the dark today: my brother, Eric, who said, "I see you are suffering a lot, and I want you to know it's optional;" Suchi Reddy, who said, "Take your pick," as she pointed to a shelf of Thầy's books at a store in New York; and my dear Lisa Eaves, who said, "I've heard of a place called the Washington Mindfulness Community that sounds pretty cool." Thank you for shining a light on a new path for me. Washington Mindfulness Community and Snowflower Sangha of Madison, thank you for continuing to hold space for me.

Without my dad, Tom Hillebrand, who read (and reread and reread) the same book Suchi helped me pick out, and without my mom, Jennylee Hillebrand, who instilled and modeled commitment to a personal spiritual practice, I might have doubted I could bridge my Christian heritage and my Buddhist presence. I am proud and humbled to be your daughter.

Without our wonderful translators—Waltraud Cogan, Eric Hillebrand, Brigitte Pichot, Dorothee Racette, and Aster Da Fonseca—we probably would have misunderstood some really important things. You all gave your time graciously and enthusiastically, never adding the weight of expectation for the final product.

Without my lovely co-editor, I would not have taken a chance on the thing I had always wanted to do: produce a book. Jeanine provided the perfect combination of an idea that spoke to my heart, wisdom that kept me grounded, and drive that kept us on track. I can't imagine this journey with anyone but you.

And without my amazing wife, Angie Hickerson, who has been supportive beyond reasonable expectation, and our curious and thoughtful kids, Lucy and Ben, who asked me every week, "How's the book going?" I would not have found the space and the listening ears to hold my struggles and my excitement. Thank you for always believing we'd get this done.

Jeanine and I are also deeply grateful to our publisher, Hisae Matsuda, and the Parallax team for their enthusiastic support of this project. Special thanks to Katie Eberle for her creativity on the cover design and our editor, Miranda Perrone, for her keen eye and collaboration. This book is yet another example of the power of Sangha!

—MARY

Monastics and visitors practice the art of mindful living in the tradition of Thich Nhat Hanh at our mindfulness practice centers around the world. To reach any of these communities, or for information about how individuals, couples, and families can join in a retreat, please contact:

PLUM VILLAGE
33580 Dieulivol, France
plumvillage.org

LA MAISON DE L'INSPIR
77510 Villeneuve-sur-Bellot, France
maisondelinspir.org

HEALING SPRING MONASTERY
77510 Verdelot, France
healingspringmonastery.org

MAGNOLIA GROVE MONASTERY
Batesville, MS 38606, USA
magnoliagrovemonastery.org

BLUE CLIFF MONASTERY
Pine Bush, NY 12566, USA
bluecliffmonastery.org

DEER PARK MONASTERY
Escondido, CA 92026, USA
deerparkmonastery.org

EUROPEAN INSTITUTE OF APPLIED BUDDHISM
D-51545 Waldbröl, Germany
eiab.eu

THAILAND PLUM VILLAGE
*Nakhon Ratchasima
30130 Thailand*
thaiplumvillage.org

ASIAN INSTITUTE OF APPLIED BUDDHISM
Lantau Island, Hong Kong
pvfhk.org

STREAM ENTERING MONASTERY
Porcupine Ridge, Victoria 3461 Australia
nhapluu.org

MOUNTAIN SPRING MONASTERY
Bilpin, NSW 2758, Australia
mountainspringmonastery.org

For more information visit: *plumvillage.org*
To find an online sangha visit: *plumline.org*
For more resources, try the Plum Village app: *plumvillage.app*
Social media: *@thichnhathanh @plumvillagefrance*

PARALLAX PRESS, a nonprofit publisher founded by Zen Master Thích Nhất Hạnh, publishes books and media on the art of mindful living and Engaged Buddhism. We are committed to offering teachings that help transform suffering and injustice. Our aspiration is to contribute to collective insight and awakening, bringing about a more joyful, healthy, and compassionate society.

View our entire library at parallax.org.